MAUSOLEUM

Giovanni de' Dondi of Padua
spent his life
building a timepiece.

A unique timepiece, unsurpassed
through four hundred years.
The gearwork manifold,
elliptical wheels,
connected by driving linkage,
and the first crown-escapement:
an incredible construction.

Seven dials
showed the position of the sky
and the mute revolutions
of all planets.
An eighth face,
the plainest,
gave the hour, the day, and the year:
A.D. 1346.

Forged with his own hand:
a celestial machine.
Purposeless, ingenious, like the *Trionfi*,
a clock of words,
built by Francesco Petrarca.

But why squander your time
with my manuscript
if you are unable
to emulate me?

Duration of daylight,
nodes of lunar orbit,
movable feasts.
A mathematical engine, and also
heaven once more.
Of brass, of brass.
That's the sky we still
live under today.

The people of Padua
didn't give the clock
the time of day.
Putsch upon putsch.
Plague-carts rolled through the streets.
The bankers
settled accounts.
Food was scarce.

The origin of that machine
is problematic.
An analog computer.
A menhir. An astrarium.
Trionfi del tempo. Leftovers.
Purposeless and ingenious
like a poem of brass.

No Guggenheim sent
Francesco Petrarca checks
the first of the month.
De' Dondi had no contract
with the Pentagon.

Different predators. Different
words and wheels. But
the same sky.
That's the Dark Age we still
live in today.

How greatly this page here resembles a thousand
    other pages,
and how hard it is to be flabbergasted at that!
The identical book, not the same one. *The art
of artificial writing:* something metallic,

a well-thumbed thought of gold, of silver,
of copper, of lead. The first reproduction
must have been a coin, the first commodity
money, the start of industry. Messages

about messages: mullars, matrices, and typefaces.
The Quattrocento, something for art historians
and theologians, anathemas, auto-da-fés,
hundred years' wars, Gothic galore.

Yes, that too. But above all: progress
in mining and milling, in metallurgy
and weaponry. Not the Madonna
in the Rose Bower, but the crane and the worm
    gear.

In the darkness of his workshop, secretly
and anonymously, and pursued by high interest
    and invoices
and cash-flow crises, he pursued
his goal, as powerful as combinatorics:

using twenty-five times two metallic signs
(not counting numerals and ligatures)
to randomly assemble and multiply
all that was, is, or could be the case,

not with the aid of the reed, the stylus, or the quill,
but through the concinnity of forms,
cut in steel, beaten in copper,
cast in lead, tin, bismuth, and antimony.

All that was necessary: Arabic pumpworks,
flax and hemp culture, cloth-presses, wine-presses,
rag-mills, import-export; an arsenal
of forgotten tools: casting-ladle, chasing-chisel,

imposing-stone, tentacle, dabber, and galley;
an army of laborers, exploiters, accomplices
from Cracow to Salamanca: wire-pullers,
rag-pickers, bankers; and only then

Gensfleisch, the old mirror-maker from Mainz,
dunned by creditors, purblind, smelling
not of incense, but of varnish
and soot. He vanished in a vapor

of hot metal. This thing here, the black
on the white paper, remained behind:
The art of artificial writing,
a leaden aftertaste of the Quattrocento.

Niccolò Niccolò five-hundred-year-old brother
I place this wreath of sere words upon thy hard
skull

Just between us we have every reason for admiring
you dry and hide-bound and theory-cankered

Niccolò master of the groveling gait
ever offended official of a scruffy republic

general-staff officer, ambassador, *Lordship*, policeman
always poorly paid for your parvenu taste

A model for all historians (*If I, without overly giv-
ing offense,
may praise or disparage these events*)

Like you once, they still rummage in filthy desk-
drawers
stuffed with smashed tin soldiers and moldy dukes

A petty country squireling, you now ate *figs and
beans and dried meat
retrieved from the maggots* and were busy with
gallstones and selling wood

And as for your women, you plucked them like
partridges

on Saturday night, and your brother-brain saw
    them as *goods and chattels*

In a mousehole wherein I find no soul who recalls
my loyal services, I squabble over ten-lira gam-
    ing debts

No sweat, Niccolò, we do appreciate your merits
and we remember your great times

For instance 1502 in Pistoia, who advised the boss
To wipe out the towns, scorch the earth, deport the
    populaces?

And any resister—to the strappado with him, to
    the gibbet?
For just a few exemplary punishments are milder
    than excessive forbearance

That was a good year for Mr. Borgia, *unbeatably*
    brilliant and grand
for his ghostwriter Niccolò and the First National
City Bank of Florence

Ten years later the catastrophe, ingratitude the
    world's reward
Pensioned off at forty-three, a rancid country estate

Tears of self-pity: *For nowhere doth ingratitude*
more cheerily rear its head than in the people's
    heart

Misunderstood like any old genius, generalissimo
mounted on a molehill, peddler of eternal truths:

*This is the cycle in which all the states in the
    world*
have turned, do turn, and shall turn for evermore

Proof: history, your self-portrait, a helter-skelter
of plunderings, perjuries, and wild intrigues

After the day's burden I cast off my dirty smock,
don splendid courtly garments and betake myself
    to the colonnade of the Ancients

And at night the lyrical soul: panhandler-sonnets
    to the officiating gangster
A true Renaissance man cringes betimes

Niccolò Niccolò the finest flower of Europe,
    chockfull
of political cunning, and a fabulous conscience

You saw through your readers, Napoleon, Franco,
    Stalin, and me,
your grateful disciple, and for that you deserve our
    praises:

For your spare and stony sentences, for your cour-
    age of cowardice,
your deeply meaningful banality, and your Nuova
    Scienza

Niccolò, villain, poet, opportunist, classic,
    hangman:
you're the Old Human Being, straight out of a
    book, and so I praise your book

Brother Niccolò, I'll never forget that; and because
    your lies
so often speak the truth I curse your crooked hand.

B. de S. (1499-1590)

At eighty his eyesight grew fuzzy.
Letter from the Indian Councilor to the Viceroy.
    Edict
of the Councilor General of the Inquisition to the
    Archbishops
of Mexico and Oaxaca. *Those heathen works are*
worthless, detrimental to the Faith, and dangerous.
The manuscripts were scattered. The school
went to rack and ruin. The pox wiped out the In-
    dians.

Sometimes he wondered what he'd been all his
    life:
a battlefield raven, or a rescuer.
Arduously, on bootleg copies, he deciphered
what his pupils had once written and painted.
The old glyphs, stiff and strange. Another world,
glassy like a specimen preserved in resin.
And his lips moved slowly. He read:

The Omen
It was ten years before the Spaniards came, it was
the first sign. It was like a tongue of fire
in the sky, like a flame, as if showering
the light of dawn. It burnt broad, it shot sharp
into the air. It appeared for a full year, at night.
And when it shone, there was screaming,
everyone screamed, everyone beat his palm
on his mouth, everyone was terrified,
horrified, waiting, with dread.

He spent his life querying. He admired
what had been demolished. And the victims *(per-*
    fect philosophers
and astrologers, incomprehensibly subtle, elegant,
thoroughly skilled in all mechanical arts)—
he tried to make them speak again. His pursuit
was a science, rigorous and new.
There was no methodology. He was the first.

He invented fieldwork: Questionnaires,
interview techniques, cross-checking, teamwork.
He trained his pupils himself: Transcription rules,
grammars and glossaries. He even climbed the vol-
    canoes.
But not what he saw was what counted.
He asked the survivors, the last of the Aztecs:
What is a mountain? They dictated. The scribe
    wrote:

The Mountain
It is something high, sharp; pointed on top,
on the peak, sharp, it towers aloft;
becomes conical, round; a round mountain, low;
with many crags, craggy; steep, cracked, craggy;
earthen; with trees; grassy; with herbs; with water;
dry; jagged; with gulleys; with caves;
It has gulleys, boulders.
I climb up, I clamber up the mountain. I live
on the mountain. I was born on the mountain. No
    one
becomes a mountain. No one turns himself into
a mountain. In the end the mountain crumbles too.
Náhuatl: Everything tastes different, has different
    colors,

names, articulations. From the sun-god to the mos-
quito:
another world. (What does that expression mean:
"Another world"?) *Description of All Things
of New Spain.* He wasn't so much interested in
how alike they (and therefore we) were
as in what he didn't understand.

A science that sees a human being
as Something Different. This incomprehensible
thing is
what frightens us and is the only hope.
The first anthropologist was hellishly frightened
of his informants and their (and our) blood sac-
rifices,
lies, idols. For three hundred years his opus
would lie in darkness, banned, in the dust of the
archives.

The Cave
*There it stretches out, there it grows long and
deep,*
it widens, it narrows. It is a narrow place,
*a place of anguish. There it becomes difficult,
rough.*
It is a dreadful place, a place of death,
a place of darkness. There it becomes dark,
black. Its mouth is wide open, its maw.
It is a broad maw, a tight maw.
I go to stay in the cave for a while.
I enter. I am here. I am in the cave.

When he had landed, a tender youth, a mendicant
    monk,
brown hood, white rope, in Veracruz,
the blood bath was already over: *Now everything
    doth lie scattered*
*on the ground and nothing doth stand upright
    anymore.*
The pyramids razed, the aqueducts smashed,
and *one cannot set foot on Mexico's soil*
without stepping on an Indian corpse.

The massacre is "of course comprehensible in its
    own terms."
It can be traced back, root and branch,
with a vengeance, to a second nature, to greed and
    fervor,
mediated (we do understand one another, don't
    we,
all too well) by class situation and economy.
If the expression "another world" means anything,
it means something we cannot *trace back.*

T. B. (1546-1601)

Behind cold, arrogant eyes, under the bald
    cranium,
that pale tissue, sensitive, an electric dough.
Capriccios of evolution. See the narwhal for exam-
    ple. It has two tusks:
One tiny, the other, always the left one, grows like
    a screw
and grows, for meters and meters; furrows and
    ridges
adorn it, spiraling left, always left.

The scarab, the unicorn, the mammoth: mere
    chimeras. Or take
that carnivore: the grand seigneur, who at thirteen
    curled up his nose
at partridges, greyhounds, fox-hunting; turned his
    tail on his class
and his eyes to the sun, which darkened. Restless-
    ness, spleen,
luxury of precision: His servants followed him
    straight across Europe,
lugging a quadrant; diameter—38 feet, oak and
    brass.

Rubbed his nose, maimed in a duel over
mathematical arguments: a golden handiwork.
Rubbed his ruddy flesh on a peasant girl: eleven
    bastards.
No time for love. Instead, an abstract prey: Knowl-
    edge

at any price. On St. Martin's Day, 1572, it flared up
brighter than Venus *(I could not believe mine own
        senses),*

BCas flared up, the Tychonian star. A supernova,
a cosmic capriccio. *Thus even the everlasting
        heavenly spheres*
do change. Europe's shamans decoded the hellish
        omen:
St. Bartholomew's Night, Black Death, Armaged-
        don. He, however,
measured to the minute, reckoned his margins of
        error: *De nova stella.*
A new chimera, costly: radio telescopes, plasma
        reactors,

Big Science. The New Isle of the Blessed. Venus in
        the Øresund,
the white cliffs of Hven, a Cythera of science.
Extravaganzas: onion domes, cylindrical towers, as-
        trolabes,
sumptuous clockworks, printing presses, allegori-
        cal automatons.
The great celestial globe alone cost five thousand
        rigsdalers.
The mammoth, however, is extinct, and there's no
        such thing as unicorns.

The King of Scotland dined with the scholar. In
        the vaults,
prisoners hammered on the iron bars: Peasant rab-
        ble!
The fool crouched under the table, a dwarf, and
        drooled the truth:

It's others who hunger! From below, a dull noise,
the king growled, the *Phoenix of Astronomy*
    cleared his throat, and, softly
scraping, the clockwork kept the world-machine
    going.

The vaults of Uraniborg Castle were one big cage.
In twenty years, the egghead engraved 777 signs in
his brass globe; every cross a fixed star, and every
    fixed star
a trodden tenant farmer. Megalomania, ennui. A
    row
with the sovereign, and the diva left Denmark. A
    caravan:
dwarf, servants, bastards, and assistants. Planetary
    tables.

But above all, the instruments. Collapsible,
for *an astronomer must be a cosmopolitan; the ig-
    norance
of rulers prevents them from grasping his worth.*
A visionary took in the visionary, Rudolf of
    Prague.
A flood of gold, a flood of guests, a booby-hatch,
teeming with brown-noses, quacks, and alchemists.

At the turn of the century, a plebeian came to
    Prague, sat
at the bottom of the table, pondering. Boorish, this
    Kepler. No
money, no sextants, mauling his master *like a mad
    dog,*
sneering and stealing. The master, greedy till his
    last breath

for gold, flesh, splendor, lay in a delirium; the ser-
    vant, obscure and methodical,
deciphered the data, gave birth to his incredible
    equations,

and darkened the dead man's light forever. Two
    mutants.
Knowledge, chimerical, without knowing for what.
    Evolution ticked
in the gray tissue. Crotchets in protein. Unicorns.
    See
the narwhal, for example, and its tusk. Our at-
    tempts at explaining
are out-at-the-elbow. A weapon: against what? A
    tool:
for what? An instrument in a ritual beyond our
    ken?

T. C. (1568-1639)

1. From the Repertoire of a Philosopher

The world is an enormous organism wherein we
dwell like the worms in our bellies.
There exist, incidentally, an infinity of worlds and
untold inhabited planets.
The two main forces moving nature are heat and
cold.
Inanimate matter is inconceivable.
Even corpses are endowed with sensations and
capable of emotions.
There are no such things as supernatural
phenomena.
The magic of naked Nature is the only sacrament
and the only mystery.
Might can be founded only on knowledge, knowledge only on perception.
The state is an artificial organism, or a machine
that men have built of men.
First we must destroy and demolish, but then re-
build and plant.

2. Thirty-nine Views

A dangerous man an agent of the Turks a Utopian
Communist a megalomaniacal mendicant monk a
prophet of brainwashing a social engineer a
purebred apocalyptic a traitor to his country a
bureaucratic visionary a papal agent an obsessive-
compulsive neurotic a peculiar saint a rank oppor-

tunist an astrological dreamer a cultural revolutionary a paranoiac an ardent world-reformer a cold-blooded rationalist an acute theoretician an agent of the Spaniards a typical advocate of chiliastic ideas a fanatic of science a compulsive clerical character a late-Gothic universalist a man of progress straight out of a book an authoritarian heretic a confused enlightener a sadomasochistic zealot a fraudulent monster an agent of the French a schemer scholastic adventurer shaman martyr forerunner sectarian forerunner magician forerunner policeman

3. From Hearsay

He supposedly was a child prodigy and supposedly an itinerant rabbi instructed him in the art of Ramon Lull;

in this way he allegedly mastered the foundations of all disciplines within two weeks;

yet supposedly his acumen triggered envy, hatred, and persecutions;

an old man whom he flung to the ground in an argument accused him, so they say, of witchcraft;

his courageous frankness supposedly always made him suspect to the Spanish government;

he was also allegedly charged with heresy, and his manuscripts were supposedly stolen and handed over to the Inquisition;

finally, so it seems, he headed a gang of dissatisfied priests, monks, and bandits to massacre all the Spaniards and incite riots in Naples;

he is said to have committed lese-majesty;

he reportedly dubbed himself the New Messiah and had himself proclaimed king of Calabria;

furthermore he allegedly colluded with a heathen navy to found an independent republic;

however, one of his accomplices supposedly sold him out;

when captured, he, allegedly, although put to the torture seven times, did not confess, but pretended to have suffered from a delirium;

he supposedly was incarcerated for thirty years in Castel Sant'Elmo, writing at least thirty folios in that time;

released in old age, he (rumor has it) put in a good word for Galileo and visited Descartes in Holland;

they also say the king of France granted him a pension;

he supposedly died peacefully at seventy-one;

after his death there allegedly was a solar eclipse;

he was supposedly buried at the monastery of Saint-Jacques in Paris, but, it is said, the Jacobins, who got their name from that place, scattered his ashes, much later, to the four winds.

4. Project for a Constitution for the Republic of Naples

1. *The State is ruled by a metaphysick named Sun.*

2. The administration of the State is divided according to the virtues necessary for the community. Every magistrate is responsible for watching over one virtue.

3. *The authorities receive absolute obedience.*

4. *Crimes against the supreme magistrates are punished with death.*
5. The institution of private property is abolished.
6. *All things are held in common, and their dispensation is by the authority of the magistrates.*
7. *Magistrates receive the full-grown and fatter portion.*
8. All adults are obliged to work.
9. *The daily working time is four hours.*
10. The division between mental and manual labor is abolished.
11. *Negligence and disobedience are punished with flogging.*
12. The State is ruled according to scientific principles.
13. Science and technology are to be fostered by the State.
14. Planning and urban construction obey the laws of mathematicks.
15. Schooling is obligatory for all. Instruction is polymathick.
16. Political issues follow the principle of criticism and self-criticism.
17. *Men and women enjoy equal rights.*
18. The institution of the family is abolished.
19. *Painting one's face is punished with death.*
20. *Pederasty is punished with death.*
21. *Procreation is the concern of the State.*
22. *Copulation is to be controlled and regulated. It can take place only under the supervision of the proper magistrate.*

5. On the Biology of the Sectarian

The sectarian lives inside the State like a tapeworm in the belly of a monster.

One distinguishes between the Armed and the Unarmed Sectarian; the latter anchors himself only by means of suckers; the former also by means of hooks in his host.

The sectarian is blind and deaf.

His path is so highly subject to chance that he necessarily must be one of the most fruitful of living creatures; hence a sectarian can have very many offspring.

The sectarian reproduces by losing limbs, eggs, larvae, fins, buds, capsules, bladders, gravel.

The treatment is always difficult because when the sectarian's head remains behind, a new body quickly grows in place of the old.

Secret remedies against the sectarian are always reprehensible.

G. W. L. (1646-1716)

We don't know his feelings. The periphery seems
   proper
as in a perfect apparatus. The privy councilor's
   state coat
was covered with buckles and buttons and laces
   and sashes.
Behind the wire-wig, the switching network metal-
   lized,
in a very dense packing. Motionless motion prevailed
under the cranium. Data—recorded, encoded,
and processed and stored: *Tabulation of knowledge,*
*Monatliche Auszüge, Journal des Savants, Acta
   eruditorum*
What he left to a helpless world was a hayrick
of annals, reports, memoranda, catalogues,
miscellanea; a hurly-burly of abstracts and
   abstracts
of abstracts and abstracts of abstracts of
   abstracts. . . .

(We of the Defense Department were never happy
   with L. True,
he's a genius, no one denies that. But there's one
   imperfection:
and that's his perfection. His "human traits,"
a certain *love of money,* a *slight podagra,* are
   camouflage,

cunning loops in his program structure, tricks,
to mislead us. It very nearly worked. Proof:
So far no one in the ruling house has any suspi-
cions.
But we say openly: L. is an artifact, and presuma-
bly,
he, humming, is employed by a remote and alien
power.)

Hanover of all places, where the houses are so
cramped!
This preference for dismal boondocks, for resi-
dences
in the German provinces, dimly lit and disreputa-
ble,
in short, a taste for the inconspicuous makes you
wonder.
He collected fossil creatures and was like a pet-
rifact himself.
But, tapping, he spread his net, tested, registered.
Met Spinoza
in Amsterdam, Newton in London, Kircher in
Rome, in Basel
the Bernoullis. Chinese interests: he corresponded
with Peking. *Novissima Sinica:* On the binary
number system
and the *I Ching*. Conversations in parks about research planning,
negotiations in chancelleries. His carriage jolted
and jogged him.
a whole academy, over the cartways of Europe.

(Our files, says the CIA, yield the following picture.

Private life: none. Sexual interests: negative. Emo-
    tionally,
L. is a moron. His relations to others are as dis-
    course
and nothing else. Furthermore, the thing that
    drives you crazy
is that insane diligence. No matter what, anywhere,
any time, he reads, writes, does arithmetic. His lit-
    tle machine,
which extracts roots, is always at hand. The step-
    ped drum rotates.
Like an automaton. Like an automaton that has
    built an automaton.)

He wrote his programs himself. The algorithms
    were new:
Infinitesimal calculus, probability theory. He
    brooded over
Lullian arts, the total trip: *Characteristica univer-
    salis.*
He posited, humming, that the world-machine is
    unconscious
but reasonable. The only thing that should matter
    is
wheedling reason out of it. Oh combinatorics! Oh
    blind faith!
I Ching: One picks a few yarrows, separates the
    stalks,
and counts, and separates and counts the stalks
    and separates, and states an oracle,
a universal method with whose assistance all the
    verities

of reason can be reduced to a kind of calculation.
At the same time, this would give us a language or
    a code
for guiding reason, for breaking error.

(We suspect, however, that it is in the nature of au-
    tomatons
to optimate optimism. Harmony is their fixation.
Their consciousness, which is happy, betrays them
    without demur.
Aside from that, the commission wonders how he
came to Boolean Algebra two hundred years too
    soon,
and it replies that there can be only one explana-
    tion:
L. is an automatic astronaut, an extraterrestrial
    probe.)

He printed out a number, countless, of metaphysi-
    cal propositions
and emitted a cloud of philosophemes, containing
his sovereign mastery of *navigation, commerce,*
    manufacture:
The virtues of these things proceed from the sci-
    ence of nature
and mathematicks. The working of the ore mines
    in the Hartz, for instance,
raised problems of drainage; sprockets and buckets,
whimseys and winches didn't suffice. Even the
    ventilation failed.
So he designed ingenious man-engines, colliery-
    fans, mine-pumps,
and crossings. Moreover, he studied the enigma of
    phosphorus,

rape-seed cultivation, coinage reform; moreover he
    proposed astronomical observatories,
clearing-houses, dye-factories; moreover, feeling no
    scruples, he planned
the silver standard and the conquest of Egypt.

(The Holy Office declares: We do not share the
    qualms
concerning him; for L. is a *mere machine,*
and higher beings, whose lot it is to live on the
    earth,
are using him. A thousand invisible hands are
    thronging
and moving in the world, hands of the angels who
    employ his hands
merely *in lieu of gloves,* for purposes we do not
    divine.)

Truth very often comes to us painted, weakened.
with a pallid face, thinning hair, old hands,
or disguised, nay, depraved and deformed; moves
    rigidly
and gravely, humming like a puppet, expediently
    and consistently,
which lowers its worth and boon. I have a taste
of iron on my tongue: He finally said it himself.
He had no imagination. *But if one were to make it*
    evident
(Truth), *one could extract gold from excrement,*
    diamonds from cesspools,
and light from the darkness, and, with utter clarity
make the progress of our knowledge apparent. Ah
    yes!

Someone, anonymous, claims *he spent his final*
    days
seeking to decipher the language of angels.

C. von L. (1707-1778)

A different folly from ours: the folly of a classic.
Clear, lean, and laconic. Back then everything was
    much smaller.
He was almost a midget, *edgy, fidgety, in a whirl,*
but the amber gaze under the weighty wig
was cutting and cold: *Any accidental feature*
must be rejected. Gathering, determining, naming.
All obscure similarities were devised to the shame
of science. Terminological knives, for the flesh
of a blind and writhing world, to peel out the con-
    stancy.

Inventories, nomenclatures, repertories. Nature
a timeless rectangle, a motionless grid.
Hand-colored prints, family-trees, tables of the law.
This language stands still in the froth of phe-
    nomena.
A grammar of gaugeables: As thick as a hair,
as deep as a navel, the shape of a vulva,
as whorled as an aurecle. Classifying,
scrupulous and "ingenious." At work night and
    day,
so that he lost no minute while staying in Uppsala:

In a lenten land, in the dingiest Dixhuitième:
a stony youth, no money for shoe-soles, food
from other plates, an always icy bed, shifts and
    dodges
for titles and talers. Finally, flight into the unin-
    habitable.

Where little could live, he was almost alive.
Lapland 1745: *Summer and winter seen on the
    same day,*
*striding through clouds, locating the end of the
    world,*
the nightly lodging of the sun. His dry heart blos-
    somed
in the cold. Reindeer-moss, tundra, arctic freedom.

Then again the court flunkies, the gardens and
    cabinets.
Hellish dreams, brooding, "ingenious" darkness.
Folly shone from the amber eyes. Immobile. At
    last,
a professor, personal physician to the Queen *(a
    happy hand*
in treating consumption), President of the Acade-
    my.
The North Star on the black ribbon. Everything too
    late.
Malaise,   suspicion,   groggy   evenings   in
    greenhouses,
then apoplexy. He spent his final four years
half-paralyzed, *in dismal debilitation of body and
    mind.*

No one knew *that he, who had found so much
    evidence*
*of God's providence among the natural objects,
    had been collecting*
similar specimens in the destinies of men;
that wonders and sins also obey taxonomy.
Persecution complex. Hallucinations. Next to the
    histoire admirable

des plantes, the natural history of diseases and
vices:

Nemesis divina, the nocturnal book, kept in a case,
full of omens, auguries, and premonitions. Reading
for Strindberg.
Empirical theology. The scientist as God's stool-
pigeon.

Everything has its order: Arson Fornication Infan-
ticide Treason
Craft and Poisoning. *Melander, Professor of Theology,*
cabaling in the consistory, until at six P.M. *his
head*
*twisted about to the back. He collapsed, was car-
ried home, never saw*
the day of recovery. God is *a timeless rectangle,*
his retribution a grid, immobile: Execution Conflagration
Defenestration Decapitation. *Mistress Psilan-
derhelm, a wanton,*
*lay with a courtier in Stockholm. An abdominal
disease,*
*she soon died. They opened her, found a stone in-
stead of a child.*

Thus everything comes to light. The sinner rots as
a living corpse.
A *fairly uniform way of life.* Punishments
gathered, determined, and named. Scrupulous and
"ingenious"
like the mechanism of reproduction: filament
pouch and pollen,

seed stylus and stigma. *Systema sexualis:* a deadly
  obsession.

Life does not exist; only living creatures exist.

Shrinking and shrinking, the grand old man
  brooded, immobile,

on a divine vendetta that would be logical. "Ingenious."

Nonsense. "Ingenious." "We" do not occur in his
  folly.

The flower named after him, Linnaea borealis L.,
is homely, tiny, and nearly all white.

J. de V. (1709-1782)

The audience was so select. A rustle
ran through the silken attire: Fantastic!
A chef-d'oeuvre: the mechanical duck.
Even Diderot was in a dither. The automaton
waddled, it paddled in water:
What delicacy in all parts!

The wings glittered in the sun,
twice four hundred movable parts.
A metallic whirring, a quacking
of steel and enamel. The artist blushed.
Modest, charming, a bit awkward.

But *the bigger and more complex a machine,*
the more connections take place
between its individual parts;
the less familiar we are with these parts,
the more ambivalent our judgment will be.

Bravo! After the *vernissage*, Cardinal de Fleury
        embraced
the inventor, and he promptly made him head
of the silk-manufactory of Lyons.
What happens when the machine
is unending in every way?

Weird, the way the new supervisor
locked himself up. Asked no one, drew feverishly.
The dream of reason gives birth to monsters:

Machines to build machines.
The power-loom, driven
by a single waterwheel (overshot)
over endless chains. *Perfection, economy.*

*The smoothened iron-wire, cut
into equal-sized lengths, and equally
bent at each end into equal links;
a hook, always the same, takes up the wire
that is meant to form the next mesh.*

From the reeling to the fullery,
an integrated industrial complex,
well lit, fully air-conditioned:
a design of unheard-of elegance.
(Certain connections take place
between profit and genius.)

From now on the workers of Lyons
spent every waking hour of their lives
in a gigantic toy,
in which they were trapped: *in such a way
that each one continually performs
the very same simple operation,
better and better, faster and faster.*

But what happens when
the weavers resist?
Smash the reeling-machines!
Stone the blood-suckers!

*To punish the rebellious mob
he constructed a mule
that wove a flowery fabric.*

And so on. *(The man who brings men*
the light of enlightenment
must be prepared for persecution.)

Then Jacquard. Jacquard was next
with his punch cards. Progress,
barricades. *The blood-baths*
were unavoidable.

The duck too was improved:
Eventually it picked up kernels,
digested them carefully, and *the stench*
spreading through the room
is unbearable. We would like to express
our delight to the artist, who gave us
such an enchanting invention.

R. di S. (1710-1771)

The coffin-makers of San Domenico still tell tall
     tales about him today,
ravens wading in sawdust,
murmur legends about vanished bodies, ballads
     blended of
magic and industry.
Ah, the inventions from the prince's boiling brain
have vanished long since!
*It would require an entire book to describe them
     accurately.*

For years he locked himself up. In his kilns, matter
     dreamt
about metamorphoses.
Then he emerged with fireworks. On the pyrotech-
     nical stage,
the flames,
in fabulous vistas, showed palaces, loggias, foun-
     tains, and trees,
flashing into the sky,
and the rockets *did artificially emulate the chirp-
     ing of birds.*

Wavering between the useful and the wondrous,
     augural,
shrewd and bizarre.
he bleached an amethyst into a diamond, fired
     lapis lazuli from marble,
marble from resin;

from *dogbane, which grows in abundance here, he
        produces the finest silk,*
plus hats, and leather
for shoes, as well as paper. One cannot desire
        more from a plant.

Five colors printed from one plate, and at one
        swoop (but we
don't believe everything);
a Neptunian vehicle, which, majestic, plowed
the sea on its own,
without any visible driving force; the king was
highly surprised
upon seeing the wagon run out on the water (we
        do not doubt it).

This science was like a drug. From cinnabar and
        quicksilver,
gold and mother-o'-pearl,
he made the blood of the saints flow forth, in
        psychedelic colors.
Others say:
He knew how to make sea-water completely sweet.
A charlatan, then?
Crumbs for bookworms. "Cultural History." *Pot
        pourri putrescence.*   (

But what stares at us in the master's crypt is evi-
        dence:
the two skeletons,
in the coppery luxuriance of a vascular plexus,
        metallized bodies,
enigmatic, violet.

preserved down to the tiniest capillaries of the
   eyeball and the kidney.
All that's certain
is that they fell into his hands alive. A monster,
   then?

An allegory, in marble, he stands, ensnared in a
   marble net,
in front of his palace.
But who is the angel next to him, the putto with
   the torch, who
 conceals him, reveals him,

freed of his folly or entangled therein? Who, in
   this harsh
glaring light
is the sorcerer? Who the deceived? Who the il-
   luminated? Who the deceiver?

1. The Marionettes

All these engravings, from changing perspectives, show a single gigantic stage, so huge and involved, that the players, like midgets, are lost in its depths. Decide for yourself, reader, whether these are cavaliers, courtesans, idlers, and gamblers, characters out of Goldoni's theater, greeting from the dizzying galleries, or artificial figures, puppets, mechanical toys. The light in which they reel over the stairs is hazy, and they look as if they, tightrope-walkers, were edging along the verge of a chasm. We do not know what play is being mounted in front of these boundless vistas.

Venezia Serenissima. The republic is bankrupt. No decline was ever merrier; commerce is sinking, pleasure is rising. Masquerades, echo concerts, extravaganzas.

Our artist, a young man (they appreciated the gondolas, clocks, and theater machines he had designed), left town and headed for Rome.

Rome was dark, dingy, and crowded; for its only livelihood was saving souls. Entering through the Porta del Popolo, the traveler saw, not crinolines and tuxedos, but mule-drivers, thieves, hunchbacks, cripples, and mendicant monks. For reasons we do not know, he settled down and engraved what he saw, in copper.

2. Archeology

What you see on these pictures are no backdrops. These buildings are not canvas. They are very much stone: marble, basalt, granite. Can't you see how heavy they are? That doesn't smell of glue. These temples and aqueducts, hot springs and colonnades must have been perfect. Now they are alien and bleak; memories cleave to them, or premonitions. They seem to bear witness to some catastrophe. And these specks straying through them—they must be beggars, washerwomen, street arabs. We do not know what these vaults signify.

Archeology: a new concept in Europe, a new madness. The past is salvaged, plundered. Antiquity is a utopia. It is excavated and reproduced. Tourists buy copies. Classicism erects the ruins of the future.

Our artist dealt in old curiosities. He published a catalogue: *Antique vases, truncated columns, sarcophagi, tripods, oil lamps, and ornaments.*

The quarry of history released a flood of counterfeits.

3. Carceri d'Invenzione

You're mistaken; these pictures do not show monuments. These are cells; for this stone interior has no exterior. The walls are impenetrable. Perhaps you haven't noticed that there are bars here and oubliettes. The world is a dungeon, a Bastille. Although light is descending (hard to say from where), this prison seems to lie under the earth; and from crenels and merlons, far, far away, guards are staring, as tiny as insects, at the inmates. Or haven't you noticed them? However, we do not know who is imprisoned here or why.

A century that thinks about liberation and phantasizes prisons. The dungeon as an obsession.

The humanitarian, a new phenomenon, remarks that the penitentiaries, *spread throughout Europe, harbor vagabonds, shirkers, beggars, as well as debauched wenches, refractory menials, naughty children, criminals, lunatics, and invalids.*

4. Torture and Industry

No, this is no jail. It must be a workshop. People work here. You musn't overlook the large tools, the winches, ramps, and trestles. Cranes move in these halls, chains crunch, cranks and wheels turn. A fire is glowing there, steam is rising. The place looks like a smithy. Only the nails are hard to explain, the poles; and those wooden constructions—we do not know whether they're scaffolds for killing or building.

The similarity between the torture instruments of an era and its technological implements.

First Degree, the crushing of the thumbs in vises that are indented or equipped with dull points: the Bamberg Torture.

Second Degree, the violent tying of the arms with hair cords and the screwing together of the legs: the Mecklenburg Instrument.

Third Degree, stretching the body out on a bench or ladder, exacerbated by burning the sides, the arms, and the nails: the "larded hare."

Torture was thus maintained in German courts of law until the end of the eighteenth century and in part even longer.

5. The Brain

You're wrong about these engravings. Just look at the light-rays and shadows, they betoken something else. Can't you see that this room, although closed, is endless? The labyrinth it pictures is your consciousness. That's why you're dizzy; because you're looking into your own brain; but we do not know what the brain is and what the consciousness is.

Now the preparators get to work: Malpighi, Vicq d'Azyr, Haller, and Reil. Anatomy too has its theater, the corpse lies on stage. The dissection of the brain reveals the following:

Fossa, the trench. *Aquaeductus*, the aqueduct. *Truncus corporis callossa*, the rafters. *Tectum*, the roofplate. *Claustrum*, the outer wall. *Fornix*, the vault. Brain researchers, philanthropists, torturers, archeologists, and puppets. How greatly the scalpel resembles the burin, the lancet the artist's burnisher! And doesn't his drypoint look just like a probe? How singular!

6. The Hallucination

You get lost in these optical illusions, these crosshatchings. You dream. That's no brain. That's a feverish raving, a delirium. Soon you yourself will resemble the insect reeling over the endless stairways, balancing on the parapets. What you see on

these engravings is another world, and we do not
know what it means.

I think that if I were assigned the task of planning a new universe, I would be crazy enough to
try it.

L. S. (1729-1799)

The abbé, high-handed, *small chin, piercing eyes,*
an electric temperament, but rather fat, climbed
     Vesuvius,
scraped in the crater-field to incorporate the fresh
     lava

in his infamous cabinet, with its tripe, malforma-
     tions,
worms in bottles. It smelled of spirits, rotten flesh.
Sulphurous fumes mingled in the pungent, rancid
     vapors.

Reflecting on a class of questions not previously
     conceived,
he found the answers by acting systematically: Sys-
     tematically,
he wielded the bone-scissors, the scalpel, red-hot
     needles. Where

does the bat fly when blinded? The brain of the
     slaughtered cow,
the muscles of the dead dog, and the lung of the
     drunken woman
kept breathing under the bell-jar for hours. *Eureka!*

I cried, overwhelmed by this unexpected joy.
Amputate parts of the salamander, shoo away the
     carrion flies,
amputate and amputate and amputate and ampu-
     tate again:

Do the tail and the legs and the jaw grow back,
     even a fifth time?
Divide the earthworm lengthwise and crosswise, in
     five parts. Off with its head.
Determine the consequences of these actions care-
     fully.

The more thoroughly you study this creature, the
     more
wondrous it will appear to you. You will wrest
     new sides from it,
so fabulous that henceforth people will say: As
     beautiful as an earthworm.

His polemics were feared. Ruthless rancor in foot-
     notes,
venomous dispute. The scholars like scorpions
     lurked for one another,
stung suddenly, and then chintzily basked in their
     victory.

Experimental reflex: *On the Digestive Behavior of*
     Man
and Various Animal Species. Take a sponge, tie it
to a thread, swallow it, haul the gastric juice from
     your body.

Tear a cat's stomach out after it's eaten, sew up the
     organ,
place it in warm water, and thus, on the table,
     demonstrate
the digestion of corpses. *Nothing could be more*
     beautiful.

An enlightened century. But swarming with
   carrion-flies.
The Abbé was a sex offender. He coupled newts
   and toads:
monstrous unions. He removed the roe from
   opened females,

then he slaughtered males, tapped their milk, and
   reproduced the dead.
This astonishing spectacle bewinged my phantasy.
(That same year, Réaumur, in Paris, constructed an
   artificial womb.)

He masturbated a dog, and injected the sperm in a
   bitch.
I can sincerely say that I have never partaken
of a keener pleasure. The creature whelped. (So did,
   shortly, the first woman.)

Rather fat, an electric temperament, a small chin:
Such descriptions do not say much, as little as our
   nausea.
The fermenting gelatine reeks, the greenish slime
   clogs in the phial,
the unexpected joy is astir, and the flies perch
on the smeared instruments. Man went about his
   business
systematically, a species striding forward *jubi-
lantly.* Eureka!

*Determine the consequences of these actions care-
   fully.*

C. M. (1730-1817)

M. The letter M on the astral maps: M 42
in Orion; M 57, the ring nebula in Lyra; plus the
    Pleiades,
M 45; and the New Star of the Chinese, the super-
    nova, M 1:
glowing clouds of gas, cosmic bombs, radio
    sources.
Al-Sûfi, heavenly falcon! Oh Swedenborg, ex-
    tragalactic dreamer!

This man in contrast: deft, clean, plain.
Starving. In Paris at twenty-one, he brought along
a pretty penmanship, and that was all.
Five hundred francs a year, plus room and board.
Delisle had him copy his plan of Peking

and his sketches of the Great Wall.
An ignoramus. He wasted eighteen months looking
for his first comet: Halley's reckonings
were inaccurate (perturbations due to Jupiter's
    mass).
Later, the king called him *the comet-ferret.*

Once his wife cost him an entire night:
She lay dying. He wept for the comet
he'd missed. While old Herschel in London
cast, polished, and mounted his gigantic refractor,
he burnt his measly midnight oil, without theories.
    An ignoramus.

Sharp eyes, a pendulum clock. A small quadrant,
a shabby telescope (seven inches). That was all.

He never slept. He sought. Eclipses, sunspots.
In an autumn night two hundred years ago
he noticed, not far from Zerta Tauri, a feeble glow.

A comet that was no comet, for it didn't move.
The phenomenon, a milky way, bothered him. He
      saw,
noted, grasped nothing. Fellow of the Royal Soci-
      ety,
the Academies of St. Petersburg and Berlin, Stock-
      holm,
finally Paris. A bookkeeper, a copyist. How blind
      he was!

Parades and processions passed under his window,
weddings and cortèges. History hollered
on Rue Saint-Jacques. The hookers beckoned, shots
      cracked,
tirades surged and subsided: Virtue, terror, and for-
      tune.
Blind and deaf. The pen scratched. Oil was short.

He didn't miss the beheaded king, nor the beer-
      brewers
and the washerwomen, the rat-catchers and the
      bankers
that the stoical ax sliced up. The astronomers
had fled. He only found one, Bochard de Saron,
a friend of Laplace. The Conciergerie stank of piss.

In his cell, de Saron figured out a comet's path for
    him
before mounting the scaffold. Then the old man
    once again
sat in the Hôtel de Cluny, unpaid, sleepless, un-
    noticed, gouty.
The city was dark. Fear, hunger, usury, inflation.
A fifteen-minute pause, then again the scraping of
    the pen.
Catalogue des nébuleuses et des amas d'étoiles
que l'on découvre parmi les étoiles fixes. Obsti-
    nate,
gentle, and reckless, like a child.
Only a letter reminds us of him. M
was an ignoramus. Two million light-years from
    here
a milky way is waning slower than we.
M 31. The smog permitting, when I look away
from the glare of Manhattan Island, from history,
I sight it, tiny, with my naked eye, in the northern
    sky,
between Mirach, Sirrah, and Shedir, in Andromeda.

J. I. G. (1738-1814)

I Legend

1) the scaffold 1a) the planks 1b) the posts 1c) the rabbets 1d) the copper sheathings 1e) the crossbar 1f) the braces

2) the knife 2a) the blade 2b) the drop-iron

3) the hole

4) the block 4a) the drop 4b) the reel-bed 4c) the trough

5) the wicker-basket 5a) the zinc lining 5b) the sawdust

6) the drawing-line 6a) the rope 6b) the tension-spring 6c) the goat's-foot-lever 6d) the catch

II Stations of a Free-Mason

Sharp-nosed, lubberly, *a moderate man all his life.*
Mysteries from the picture-book: Bare-chested,
    blindfolded,
he was led to the lodge by the brothers. One foot
    naked, the other shod,
first the beaker of bitterness, then the incense, the
    swords;
first the darkness, then the light: Le Grand Orient
    de France.
Liberty, humanity, equality, sublime masquerades.
The dissertation of a humanitarian: *How to fore-*
    stall
the effects of rabies. (Rabies is other people.) Fear
of the mob, the riffraff lurking outside. In his
    cabinet,

the fashionable physician fiddled around with lan-
cets, cupping-glasses, leeches.
A clumsy speaker, mediocre; pleaded his cause
with bombast:
*With my machine, messieurs, I can dispatch you
from this world*
in a jiffy without your feeling any pain. Laughter
in the assembly, then silence, finally resolutions,
reports, rough estimates.

III A Mechanician from Germany
*Citizen-deputies, by trade I, Tobias Schmidt, am a
builder*
*of mechanical musical instruments; yet I some-
times forsake this art*
*in favor of new inventions, which I consecrate to
the benefit of mankind.*
My hydraulic machine permits diving to any depths,
*to saw under water, to nail, to bore, to salvage lost
objects*
*from the bottom, to tarry in the depth for half a
day*
while conversing with the dry land. Furthermore,
*I most humbly offer you a draw-ladder for saving
people*
*from a conflagration, and as for my piano, it pro-
duces tones*
*and blows notes in such a way that one imagines
one is hearing*
now a violin, now a bass, now an alto voice.
Schmidt, a periodic tippler,
was the lowest bidder: three hundred and twenty-
nine francs.

IV Ingratitude

The first try-outs in the merchants' exchange, Rue
    Saint André-des-Arts, on live sheep.
The headsman was a traditionalist, a blockhead,
    hard to enlighten.
Later, in the grand amphitheater of the Hospital of
    Bicêtre,
five fresh corpses. A total triumph: *The mechanism*
falls like a thunder-bolt, the blood spurts, the man
    is no more.
The humanitarian died, pious, rich, pale, in bed,
    many decades later,
with all possible sacraments. *But as ill fortune*
    would have it,
the ignorant mob linked his illustrious name for
    all time
to the instrument. . . . Let us thus bear in mind
    how difficult it is
to do good unto others without their requiting
the bestowal of such a boon with evil.

A. C. de C. (1743-1794)

Kindness shone from his eyes. Seemingly al-
    together (like Schlemihl)
shadowless: reasonable, noble, the pride of science,
    an aristocrat, true,
*but the love of humanity soon led him on the path
    of revolution.*
In his final hideout, he wrote *The Light* shortly be-
    fore the end *of the Enlightenment guarantees
    that we* in the glow of a candle-stub
are advancing towards a happy future. Your
    money or your life: How sad
that the Citizen Marquis lost both at once. Our
    condolences. Yet
terror is always a tic-tac-toe: a stochastic game.

For the moment he was known as skillful and cool.
    Inspector of the Mint,
Navigation Director, Permanent Secretary of the
    Academy. His career moderate
but versatile, mindful of the collective good.
    Studied the theory
of comets, the three-body problem, and trade statis-
    tics.
*However his ever-aspiring mind indulged in
    suggestions
more than completions.* Aha! Suggestions! Get the
    arrest warrant.
He went underground, condemned to death. No
    wonder. Anyone that virtuous,

that liberal, with that fine a background, is usually
the first to be liquidated.

The customary epithets from the repertoire of
obituaries and eulogies:
"lofty intellect," "great sensitivity," "loving hus-
band and father." Certainly, certainly.
Only the parlando of praise leaves all kinds of
questions open. E.g.,
the white ribbon in his hair: Is it true that his
mother
sanctimoniously dedicated him to the Holy Virgin,
and that he went among prelates,
until he was fifteen, in coifs and crinolines, pick-
led in prayers?
Was that a reason, and if so, how, that this timid
man,
rosy and distinguished, became the forebear of the
coarsest technocrats?

In the realm of experience, probability rules, i.e.,
statecraft,
the will of the people, commerce and industry are
a kind of tic-tac-toe
for which we must find mathematical models.
Breakage and shrinkage
can now be calculated, and the shamans of theory
instruct us henceforth
*In the advantage that he who knows how to calcu-
late his game*
can gain over the man who relies on instinct
or on routine. We are much obliged for Markov
machines

and for the Minimax principle: We shake the hand
  of the Citizen Marquis.

He cheated the guillotine. But if it's true he was
  found in his cell,
*killed by a poison he had been carrying for some
  time,* what can we conclude
in regard to his *Tableau of the Progress of the
  Human Mind?*
Dabber of philosophical white, sentences as soft as
  cotton. Could he have
written them with the poison on this tongue? In-
  hale with care.
Barbarity is conquered forever. A naive fluid rises
  into our noses,
and we wonder just what this philosophy is all
  about:
Is it an evocation, a fragrant scorn, a fervent
  prayer, an *idée fixe,* or a bluff?

O. E. (1755-1819)

I

A Mill is a Machine in which Wheelworks, driven by some external Power, are used to grind or crush a Substance. If the word Mill is unmodified by any attribute, it is generally construed to signify a Flour-Mill. . . . Mills are a very ancient Invention.

II

One bright July morning early in the last century, the citizens of Philadelphia, a bucolic settlement on the Delaware River, were treated to the following spectacle.

A conveyance, twelve by thirty feet, appeared on Center Square; it carried an iron boiler immured in brickwork, a watertank, and a chimney; an engine with pistons, cranks, valves, a flywheel, and a balancing pole; moreover, a pump, an enormous paddle-wheel, and an endless belt studded with drag buckets; and this vehicle, weighing fifteen tons, encircled, without benefit of draft-horses, the round bed and the fountain for several days.

Then, to the hurrahs of the spectators, it squealed along, on its own power, down Market Street, for a mile and a half, up to the boat-landing, cast off its wheels, sank the paddles into the water, and puffed downstream until it passed out of sight.

III

The constructor, a burly man with a bluish red face, stood on the bank and laughed. Except for his being a choleric, we know little about him. All his works are moldy and rusty, and his papers, drawings, and plans—he burnt them all. He plays a vital role in the history of bread.

IV

Many of the words he used (he was a trained wainwright) are obsolete: thill, sway-bar, dish, dash-guard. A turned-up tester—he could have explained what that is.

V

...*a species that systematically guides its own development by methodically influencing its living conditions and its genetic program. This process is known as* auto-evolution. (Example: The wainwright who goes under as a wainwright by inventing a steam-wagon. The miller too does not die out on his own.) The final purpose that every finality pursues is unknown.

VI

From the cartload the grist is brought to the scale and then to the screw conveyor; from there it comes to the stone-floor, flowing through the chute into the shaking-shoe; it runs from the shoe, past the rynd, and is pressed between the wolfstone and the bedstone into the hoop, moves through the scuttle into the bolter, lands in the sifting-chest, passes to the threshing-floor, under the gyrating sifter, continues into the mixing-chamber, gathers on the flour-floor, courses through the filling tube into the bin. The mill teems with perspiring millers; with mill-masters, mill-clients, mill-hands; incessantly they move the groats, the cutlings, the middlings, the sharps, the first patent, second patent, straight grade, first clear, second clear, red dog; they heave and haul, they shovel and lug about and about.

Then the inventor appears and erects a mill from which the millers disappear. All that moves in the deserted building is lifts, elevators, conveyors, descenders: *Apparatuses with which the Substance, in part horizontally, in part vertically, passes from one device to the next through the Machine so that any Manual Labour or Impurification are forestalled.*

VII

Flow charts, process computers; band production, process engineering. A coordinated wheelworks, a very ancient invention, driven by some internal power. A mill, but no more miller.

T. R. M. (1766-1834)

After not eating for a long time, you're too weak to
    talk,
you poke about in garbage, stop writing. What we
    know about hunger
comes from the tongues of the sated; so it's not
    much.

The merriest of men: summertime, a little rowing;
    wintertime,
skating on the village pond. *In fifty years
I never once saw him lose his temper.*

Chubby-cheeked, sluggish, his firm voice con-
    tradicted fortune.
His fortune? Fortune. It was no longer *a new idea
in Europe: There will be no wars, no crimes, no
    administration
of justice, and no government. Besides this, no dis-
    ease, anguish,
melancholy, nor resentment.* Answer: *I had not ac-
    quired that command
over my understanding which would enable me to
    believe what I wished
without evidence. (An Essay on the Principle of
    Population
As it Affects the Future Improvement of Society,
with Remarks on the Speculations of Mr. Godwin
    and M. Condorcet.)*

Sweetness of temper, tenderness of heart. Genius
and madness were nothing for him.

Earned an honest living from his sinecure, but
Süssmilch's

Divine Order in the Changes of the Human Race
did not put

his mind at ease. So he thumbed Statistical Year-
books,

left his vicarage, traveled to Russia and other
places.

All Europe was shocked by the result. Monotonous
evocations:

that *whole train of common diseases and
epidemicks,*

dearth, wars, plague, and famine.

The pastor of the good people of Albury got hot
and bothered

at the *irregular gratifications, improper arts,*

unnatural passions; but his folio for the first time
reckoned

the natural force in wombs and testes, just as the
physicist figured out

the velocity and range of a projecticle passing

through resisting media of different densities: all
this

is necessary, and will forever continue to exist.

Shameless sycophant of the ruling classes, vile,

infamous theory, cynicism, revolting blasphemy:
Easily said,

but now as ever the doubling time

is around thirty years, and now as ever: $P_t = P_0 e^{rt}$.

Granted, his reckonings weren't good enough. All
    he knew was:
Something grows, becomes more, more and more.
    Growth grows too,
hunger grows too, so does fear. With rosy cheeks
he sat down to tea, rubbing his hands, had the
    muffins served
by a rosy woman, always the same, whom he,
    modest and prudish,
had sex with once a month: intrepidly chicken,
a malingerer, who played the healthy man all his
    life.
Among the prophets of catastrophe: *the merriest of*
    men.

A. von H. (1769-1859)

Outside, painted in oil and very blue, the faraway
    peaks, the palms,
the naked savages: inside, in the shade of the leafy
    hut,
the walls hung with skins and giant ferns, a gaudy
    macaw
perched on the pack-saddle, the companion in the
    background held a blossom
under the magnifier, orchids were strewn on the
    crates of books,
the table was covered the plantains, maps, and in-
    struments:
the artificial horizon, the compass, the microscope,
    the theodolite,
and shiny brassy, the reflecting sextant with the
    silvery limbus;
bright in the middle, on his camp-chair, sat the
    celebrated geognost
in his laboratory, in the jungle, in oil, on the banks
    of the Orinoco.

The terra incognita melted like snow under his
    gazes.
He cast his net of curves and coordinates over the
    last glaciers,
the bleakest mountains. He measured the magnetic
    variation,
the sun's altitude, the salt content, and the blue of
    the sky. Incredulous,

the natives watched him. What *wonderful people*
    they are,
who traverse the world to seek plants and compare
    their hay
with other hay! *Why do you let yourselves be de-*
    voured by mosquitoes,
merely to get the lay of land that doesn't even be-
    long to you?
They're foreigners, heretics and fools. But as un-
    waveringly as the cleric
waves his censer, the voyager wields his Leyden
    jar.

Born in the blaze of Messier's Comet, he gal-
    vanized frogs,
put electrodes on himself and reported *Conjectures*
    on [his]
Irritated Nervous and Muscular Fibers. Later, he
    chased after
electric storms on the Amazon and northern lights
    in Siberia: pirogues
carried him there, sleighs and steamers, hammocks
    and coaches.
He depicted *entire lands as a mine.* A vulcanist
    and vulcanologist,
he had a genuine mania for burning craters, which
    he passionately
climbed, surveyed, and examined. Isolated and an-
    xious,
he recalled the youths he had liked. Most of them
    were gentle
and penniless. He helped them, however, and held
    his tongue. The agonizing nights

were devoted to writing. *Random Remarks on Basalt.*

On Quinquina Forests. A Memoir on Ocean Currents. On the Native Populations
of *America and the Monuments they Left Behind.*
Lectures on. . . . Contributions to. . . . Aphorisms from. . . . and Views concerning. . . .
Provisional Note on a Life-saving Bottle. On the Lower Borders
of *Perpetual Snow. On the Temperature Occurring on the Ocean Surface*
in *Various Parts of the Torrid Zone. On Electrical Fish.*
This man is a perfect walking academy. He mounted
to the highest layers of air, and, in an iron bell,
with a lunatic Briton named Brunel, he dived to the bottom of the Thames.

I always admired him: now I worship him. For he alone
offers *a notion of the feelings aroused in the soul*
when *arriving in the Tropics.* Later, however, after breakfast,
Darwin was *rather disappointed: I found him to be very cheerful,*
but *he talked too much.* In point of fact, the basis of his greatness
is not quite clear. He slept only three or four hours, he was vain,
enthusiastic, innocuous, *infinitely busy. An excellent dancer,*
from the minuet to the animalito.

Blue tails, gold buttons, the waistcoat
yellow, striped trousers, a white cravat, a black,
worn-out hat:
his wardrobe had stopped in the days of the Di-
rectoire.

A celebrity back then: *Scarcely has any private*
gentleman
ever provoked a greater sensation. Paris in sus-
pense: the New Class still didn't trust
its own triumph. Deceptive, a classicistic inno-
cence blossomed
after the Terror, before the bestial bellowing of
brokers
filled the *Bourse* with frenzy, boom, crash, and *the*
open, shameless,
direct, brutal exploitation raced over the entire
globe. . . . A lucid moment
clean and homogenous. The Bourgeoisie acted
exemplary and cool
like the primal meter. Even our noble hero con-
tributed a mite
to determining it and, with his instruments,
traveled the meridian
of Dunkirk-Barcelona. (As usual, he paid the ex-
penses out of his own pocket.)

Then the reactionaries won. Back to German
wretchedness. A gentleman-
in-waiting, a reader, i.e., flunky at Potsdam's court.
He secluded himself in Berlin,
a *tiny, intellectually desolate, overly malevolent*
town. In this heavily policed

sandy waste, he often thought about the Tropics.
　　Why were they so bewitching?
Why had he endured it all: insects, lianas,
　　downpours,
and *the sullen gazes of the Indians?* It wasn't the
　　tin, the jute,
the rubber, the copper. A healthy man he, an un-
　　witting carrier
of the disease, a selfless harbinger of plundering, a
　　courier
who didn't realize he had come to announce the
　　annihilation
of what he lovingly painted until ninety, in his
　　Views of Nature.

Did you see the mealy minds in the shops,
and, in the offices, the tired copyists and commer-
    cial clerks,
with their sleeve-protectors, sand-holders, and
    erasing-knives,
the way they sit, declassé for all time, full of ink
    splotches
and forever fettered to their tills and desks?
The century of colonial goods and competition
teemed with them, needed them, and paid them no
    heed.

Just imagine his cold bed and harsh breakfast
and consider how punctual he is, how furnished,
    and that these
are his pleasures: a game of billiards Saturday
    night,
a talk with the cat, pruning and watering the
    plants.
Yet, his home looks like a hothouse, a winter-
    garden.
Order prevails among the indoor palms, and sym-
    metry, and heavily,
like the smell of hashish, a heavy green odor hov-
    ers in the air.

With *Hannibalistic curses* he cursed commerce,
    but why bother!
For in Rouen, he submitted bales of cloth to his
    clientele,

in Marseilles he sold spices, reeled off price-lists in
    Lyons,
railed against stone brokers in the curb market and
    cooed
offers, as a traveler he walked the streets, gripped
    doorknobs,
weighed bags and, in Paris, with his fantastic quill,
    he had
to scratch figures and names in other people's
    demand-deposits.

Kepler, he said, *and I.* And then one day in
    obscure gazettes
he announced his discovery: *the gravitation of the
    passions,*
*Universal Harmony, the enigma of the four move-
    ments,*
*the mathematically proven determination of all ce-
    lestial bodies*
and their inhabitants, and the opening of a univer-
    sal era of happiness.
Columbus, Newton, Descartes, and I: Do you hear?
    Here comes the fool!
the schoolboys shouted after him in the gardens of
    the Palais Royal.

But make no mistake: he was no "Critic of Soci-
    ety,"
he was its foe. Fabula rasa, or *The Absolute Devia-
    tion.*
That was the least. That had to be. For *the pas-
    sions*

are *always right*, and *our mistake is not so much*
    asking too much
as too little. Do you hear? *His peculiar oeuvre,*
    containing,
along with a mass of nonsense, frequent highly in-
    tellectual
notions in dark language, promises, for the future,
orgasms and blossoms, benefit and pomp, melons
    and adventures.

Just see how seriously he studies! He loves science,
despises lies. And on all his travels he took a
    yardstick
for measuring gardens and squares. He spoke about
    everything, understood
everything, and kept accounts on everything. What
    does opera mean,
cauliflower, and gold? What is the tapeworm? The
    Milky Way?
Free-Masonry? Siberian ice? The bat and the
    comet?
Swedenborg, he said, and I, and sank into al-
    legories.

But what did he do with his madly meticulous ta-
    bles,
with his raving enumerations, with his mouse-
    eaten
manuscripts on *The New World of Industry and
    Love?*

He gave them to you! Do you understand? He gave
    you his calculations

his well-ordered orgies and systematic fruit-cakes,
here they are, take his ceremonial ecstasies,
his erotic glossolalia, and eat, and fuck, and drink!

Away, he shouted, away with ennui! Monogamy!
    Censorship!
Fear! Duty! And poverty! Down, do you hear, do
    you understand,
with asceticism! Hierarchy! And industrial hell!
He hollered, he yelled, he stammered and stuttered
    in his threadbare jacket
under the indoor linden tree, babbling exactitude,
    and suddenly
the paradisal machinery started, the springs and
    cams started,
and the gears, worm wheels, and connecting rods
    of passionate harmony

started moving all by themselves, wonderfully, ef-
    fortlessly. Look!
Can you see them now! Whirling and swirling,
    higgledy-piggledy, dancing
in perfect order, happy, his creatures: Fairies
and fakirs, genies, angels of love, magnates, bac-
    chantes, heroines,
sybils, vestal virgins, seraphs, paladins, and
    courtesans.
Now he glows, flaunts his unknowingness, boasts
that nobody knows him, the Prophet, the *Pariah of
    Science.*

For *a shop sergeant shall shatter the cabal*
of philosophers and give the lie to the four
    hundred thousand
books of the hypocrites. (How deliciously confused
    he is! How sublimely ridiculous!
How cunningly naive!) *But would it not be desira-*
    ble, he asked
that I be right and all others wrong? And uninter-
    ruptedly
he wrote to princes, tsars, ministers, ambassadors,
    and bankers,
sending them his illegible petitions, applications,
    manifestoes.

So long live, he wrote ceremoniously, *drives and*
    whims,
nay, even quirks and manias! But soon came
    winter,
they stole his ideas. *Lust,* he scribbled, *long*
    live. . . .
The flattery of disciples was stifling. *Long live*
debauchery! But he didn't trust them. *Luxury,*
    superabundance!
Cold and thoughtful he raged against riffraff; em-
    bittered,
he isolated and repeated himself, embroiled in the
    wildest tirades.

Silence resounded against him. Observe him carefully,
the way he listens! Did someone ring, knock? Imagine:
inflexible and silent like Bartleby, with open eyes,
or like Pécuchet at his desk, proud and immodest,
he'll be found
by the concierge one morning, under the leaves,
dead,
kneeling, on the fifth floor, on Rue Jean-Jacques
Rousseau,
between potted plants, in a stupefying green smell
of spent seed.

C. B. (1792-1871)

Of a somewhat eccentric nature. Massive, irascible,
     helpless:
a dyed-in-the-wool bachelor with aching ears.
waving his cane, he pursued a mob
of urchins, trumpeters, and hurdy-gurdy men.
He flinched before his niece: an embroidery-frame
on pale girlish knees. No biographer mentions
those heated dreams of steam-engines and golden
     curls.

Once, holding his mother's hand, he saw,
in a brightly lit house on Hanover Square,
an automaton of Vaucanson's (The Metallic Bal-
     lerina),
and the gears began moving. A grating
in the boy's brain, a gentle steady grating.
For seventy years the mechanism never stood still.

Problems: *Compute the relative frequency of oc-
     currence*
of the causes of breaking plate glass windows;
enumerate the possibility of having
a man stand up from the dead (solution: $1:10^{12}$);
*arrange twenty thousand needles, thrown promis-
     cuously*
into a box, with their points all facing one way;
find a method of creating facsimiles
of any products of nature or human industry.

His travels through Europe in a coach of his own
    devising,
in which he could sleep and boil eggs; its shelves
    contained
construction plans, dress-coats, telescopes, plus a
    stomach-pump.
His expedition to Mount Vesuvius: a phial of smel-
    ling salts,
a walking-stick that burst into flames: reminis-
    cences
of Spallanzani's wanderings and of Romanticism.

But when poor Tennyson sent him his verses
(*Every minute dies a man / Every minute one is
    born*),
he suggested that *in the next edition of your excel-
    lent poem*
*the erroneous calculation should be corrected as
    follows:*
*Every minute dies a man / And one and a sixteenth
    is born.*

He will presently invent a Novel-writing machine,
said Emerson. And he: *The pig fair at Pavia and
    the book fair*
at Leipsic equally placed before me menageries.

The automaton he built instead cast no literature
up, but logarithms. Every time the device
hit upon an imaginary root, a bell rang.

Eighteen hundred thirty-four, the year of Büchner's
     Hessian Courier,
Charles Babbage, obsessive-compulsive, Fellow
of the Royal Society, founder of operations
     analysis,
conceived the punch card.

He hair-split pin-making into seven different parts:
drawing straightening pointing twisting heading
     tinning papering,
computing the wages expended in millionths of a
     penny.
A few stone's throws from Mr. Babbage's hearth, a
     Communist
sat in the British Museum, checking the arithmetic
     and finding it correct.
It was a foggy evening. The mills and stores of in-
     dustry
released a gentle, steady grating.

The great unfinished works: *Das Kapital* and the
     Analytical Engine.
Forty Victorian years. The first digital computer,
with no vacuum tubes, no transistor. Weighing
     fifty tons,
as big as a room, a gearwork of brass,
pewter, and steel, driven by springs and weights,
capable of any computation whatsoever, even of
     playing chess,
or composing sonatas, more than that: *to simulate
     any process*
which alters the mutual relation of two or more
     things.

Pondering over plans that covered an entire storey,
I have converted the infinity of space, required
by the conditions of the problem, into the infinity
      of time,
conditions enabling a finite machine to make
calculations of unlimited extent. That instant, someone

appeared at the door of the lab, Lady Lovelace, veil-
      ed
and explaining the purpose of these gears, worms,
and camshafts: *He weaves algebraic patterns*
on his Engine just as the Jacquard loom
weaves flowers and leaves. (She was Byron's
      daughter.)

And it was largely completed in wonderful Beauty
[the Engine] *when its construction was interrupted.*
The expenditures had risen to twenty thousand
      pounds sterling,
and since the final execution was estimated at
      twice that amount,
the project was discontinued.

And it has been lying ever since, like a mammoth,
      a quirk of evolution,
a future fossil, on the ground floor of the Ken-
      sington Museum.
A factory in which all other factories are con-
      tained. A ruin.
The howling of the hurdy-gurdies, splitting the
      ears of Mr. Babbage,

Fellow of the Royal Society, is programmed. A set
    of punch cards
grind away, determine the piecework, and reveal
    the absentees.

The wheels, set in motion in an eight-year-old's
    brain
by the sight of a silver dancer. *I doubt*
whether I ever spent a happy day in my life.

A gentle grating, in which each shriek drowns.

L. A. B. (1805-1881)

Honeycomb Cells   (1)
Sickly, puny, shriveled, a delicate constitution; an old man at forty. A mystery-monger. Brooked no contradiction. Always able to fool himself and ready to fool others.

Read a lot, spent his life in a series of cells. (Both meanings of the word.) Favorite reading: *The Prince.*

Accustomed to loneliness, carefully cultivated aloofness: *I do not adore the crocodile.* (The crocodile is the masses.)

Called himself a fatalist, but what does that mean anyway. One man keeps (fatalistically) abed, the other runs (fatalistically) amuck. The latter, as long as he lives, methodically clashes with a force, that, as long as he lives, seizes hold of all the earth. An explanation for this behavior does not occur.

An Astronomical Hypothesis   (1)
If, however, the universe is infinite, then this means that Nature day for day brings forth billions of solar systems, which are nothing else than slavish copies of ours.

We can conceive of no pebble, no tree, no animal, no human being, no event that cannot find its place in those remote duplicates.

Honeycomb Cells   (2)
Whenever he, after years of incarceration, left

prison and appeared before his adepts, *with hag-gard cheeks, his lips white, more dead than alive, in a black cloak, black gloves, which he never re-moved:* operatic, the *Chief,* the priest-king of the revolution—each time, *law and order blanched be-fore him.* He was the spawn of Establishment angst: terrorism incarnate, and the most righteous dude under the sun.

Paris, underground Paris, was a babel of sects, circles, and clubs. Initiation rituals: the blindfolded eyes, the murmured oath, the gleaming dagger in the hand. (The decorations of conspiracy come from the heritage of the Free Masons.)

In the Society of Seasons, Sunday led the week, March the Spring, Spring the year. At the tip, right at the top, dazzling, the Central Committee: a fiction.

An Astronomical Hypothesis (2)
If, however, the real earth has hosts of doubles in the universe, then this obtains even more so for each of its possible variants.

Each instant, as it were, brings new bifurcations, partings, alternatives. Whatever choice we may make, we do not escape our fate. But in terms of the universe as a whole, fatality finds no more support. The infinite knows of no either/or; for it has room for everything.

Honeycomb Cells (3)
My program? I do not know what it will look like. (The demand for higher wages was meaningless to him.) *The man who has iron, has bread.* (He loved

order.) *The State is entitled to omnipotence, the administration of everything.* (The mole grubs, burrows, undermines; but what it overthrows will arise all the more splendid.) *The secret leaven that stealthily lifts the masses, the invisible army of progress—those are the declassé.* (He now turned quite avuncular.) *The masses must be aroused to life from their deathlike sleep.*

From his officers he demanded: self-sacrifice, deepest silence, absolute obedience; and he offered them: poverty, moral danger, persecution, plus a series of inevitable defeats.

An Astronomical Hypothesis   (3)
Consequently, there exist billions of other earths, on which Man pursues roads that he scorns or misses here; and this obtains for every single one of us, for every instant whatsoever, every conceivable bifurcation, every possible alternative. We thus all have numberless doubles, variants of ourselves, and all that we might have been or become here, we really are, somewhere, on other, faraway planets.

Honeycomb Cells   (4)
The insurrection made progress, but so did the police: the *moucharderie* was refined, the files piled up, the secret funds mushroomed, provocation was developed to a fine art.

A worm gnawed at the coteries of the Bohème: everywhere splintering, intrigue, betrayal.

Even in the cell, everything was suspect. The

prisoner washed every pea, every bean, before eating it. He wondered daily why he wasn't poisoned. (Answer: *the government doesn't know what it's doing.*)

On the other hand, general-staff work, military expertise, *destructive machines of magical efficacy.* The boss, bowed over his reckonings—are they *considerably obsolete,* or are they premature?

He didn't live to see the October putsch in St. Petersburg. *(All power to the State.)* All his disciples, except for Mussolini, disavowed him.

An Astronomical Hypothesis   (4)
The life of our planet, from birth to death, is repeated day by day, with all its unhappiness, all its crimes, on myriads of sister-stars. That which we call progress stirs and passes, as though enclosed in a cage, on each of those many earths. Always and everywhere, the same drama, with the same sets, on the same narrow stage: a blustering Mankind residing in its prison as though it were a limitless universe, only to go under very soon together with the star that carries it. What monotony! The universe marks time.

Honeycomb Cells   (5)
While the Communards were being butchered, the prisoner was incarcerated at Fort Taureau, a rock in the ocean. He made no comment. He regarded the sky, a *comet graveyard.* Then, in his black clothes, he sat down at the table in his cell, took the quill, and wrote: *Eternity through the stars, or*

An Astronomical Hypothesis   (5)

What I am writing down in this instant, in a cell in Fort Taureau, I am also writing on billions of Earths and will write it through all eternity, and on a table, with a quill, and in clothes that are fully identical with mine.

J. E. R.-H. (1805-1871)

I From the Catalogue Raisonné

The Miraculous Draught of Fishes The Air Clock
     The Floating Virgin
The Inexhaustible Bottle The Fantastic Orange Tree
and The Magic Folder: The latter, a flat portfolio,
     lies
on two trestles in the middle of the stage, and the
     Master
removes: a set of etchings, two ladies' hats,
four flying doves, three big copper pans,
the first filled with beans, the second water, the
     third fire,
a cage of canaries and a slumbering youth,

II Preparing for a Spectacle

In the lobby of the theater of Algiers, cast-iron
     stucco and plush,
the governor, Marshall Randon, dressed to kill, is
     awaiting
the Berber princes, the sheiks of the Kabyls,
     Bash-Agas, and Kaïds.
The last rebellion was liquidated. Guarded by le-
     gionaires,
wearing crimson coats, signs of subjugation,
     splotched with decorations,
the natives appear, to view the marabouts of the
     occupiers.
The foreign seats are uncomfortable. The hush is
     deep.

III   A Villa in the Second Empire

The doors are spirited open, bells are ringing, flare-signals
flying, an automaton punctually feeds the horses, the alarm clock
kindles a match in the morning: Miracles of technology.
Through a hidden relay the Master turns all the clocks
back and forth at will: Lord over Time. The visitors
gape. It is easier to deceive an intelligent man
than an ignoramus. The host yawns. Precision engineering
may just be a branch of psychology. Or vice versa.

IV   Speech to the Arabs

I am going to show you that we French are vastly superior
in every way to you and your magicians. White Magic
makes me invulnerable. I can make any one of you disappear.
Let me now give you further proof of my wonderful might
by demonstrating that I can strip the strongest man
amongst you of all his strength at will. (The Arabs
merely smirked in scorn.) Do you see this cassette,
as big as a book? If you're a man, then lift it aloft.

V   On the Art of Illusion

He saw Vaucanson's duck at the Palais Royal, took it apart, found

the secret of the shit: a virtuoso exposed a virtuoso.
All Paris flocked to his theater: *Les Soirées fantas-*
    tiques.
Hoffmann's tales came true and were dis-spelled:
Trompe-l'oeil. At Buckingham Palace he demon-
    strated
his writing automaton to Her Majesty. In a dainty
    hand,
the machine replied to Victoria's questions and,
    when stumped,
it drew elegant emblems. A Turing game,
but the punch cards were marked. Reason was
    tricked
by the strict application of reason. No telling
the progress of swindle from the swindle of pro-
    gress.
The audience was awed, the applause wouldn't
    end.

VI The Electrostatic Machine

At last, exhausted, gasping, red with anger, the
    savage began
to grasp the effects of my art. Why, you're as weak
as a woman! Raging, he once again bent over the
    cassette.
His arms suffered a violent cramp, his legs buckled
    under him,
he fell to his knees with a shriek of pain:
At a wave of my hand, the hidden apparatus,
an induction coil, had given him an electric shock.
The result was a panic in the public. Never
has success so warmed the cockles of my heart.

I. K. B. (1806-1859)

Admission: One shilling. In thronged the tourists
    in the dim gaslight
and gazed at the laborers: half-naked, bestial, eight
    yards deep
under the Thames. A thousand bricks per man per
    day, up to their knees
in stinking water. The tunnel blinded a number of
    them.
But the demiurge did the longest shift: Thirty-five
    hours and a half.

A black deposit in the mouth, in the lungs: Ver-
    tigo, vomiting,
circulatory collapse. Finally, the celebration: a
    banquet under the river,
fifty guests of honor. The side arches hung with
    crimson draperies.
The Coldstream Guards played in gala dress. Toasts
    to the Queen.
A technological opera. Then the water burst in:
    Panic!

A thunderous cataract. . . . . The effect was grand.
    We were up
to our necks in the flood. Rather a gratification.
    (Six lives lost.)
Crises, Cabinet meetings, shrieks of rage in the
    Board of Directors.
Then fame overcame him. Each catastrophe a
    triumph.

Each triumph a catastrophe. Only the drowning are
    that determined.

The great engineer was short: the nerves of a giant.
A maniacal early-riser. Fifty cigars a day. He raced
from project to project in a black britzka, got out,
melancholy, a destroyer who loved Virgil's
    Eclogues, and screamed:
Everybody must be under my control. I want tools!

In the nursery, music-boxes and automatons, later
    the clockworks
and the planing machines. *The standards of preci-*
    sion must improve every day:
that was how his father said grace. *Machinery so*
    perfect
appears to act with the happy certainty of instinct
and the foresight of reason combined.

When he was six, the *Misfortune* came, never for-
    gotten,
never mentioned by name: The old man bankrupt,
    in debtor's prison.
From now on his reason ran amuck. *The capital of*
    my enterprises:
five million pounds. Not bad for a man of
    thirty. . . .
In fact I am now somebody. (Always those nagging
    doubts.)

Sluices, drydocks, giant viaducts: *Quite different*
    wonders
from Egyptian pyramids, Roman aqueducts, Gothic
    cathedrals.

Certainly. However the bridge-piers were adorned
    with finials;
brooding over the corner-arches of the chain rol-
    lers,
two sphinxes eyed one another stonily over the
    gorge.

Railroad fever. Devoured by delusions of grandeur:
    No gauge
was great enough for him. Gargantuan locomotives.
    A jungle
of committees and sub-committees. He built his
    own terminal,
Paddington, a crystal palace. Moorish ornaments
adorned the aisles. The usual jubilant yells. Bored
    stiff,

he drove home. The coach lined with black silk.
Venetian looking-glasses, grandeur à la mode. Cold
    and hysterical,
Mary Horsley. A little Chopin. Charades and balls.
    Goose pimples:
My profession is after all my only fit wife. Occa-
    sional
visits by Mr. Babbage, a guest of few words.

Gold: One night he swallowed a sovereign. Chok-
    ing, near death,
he invented a device, had himself strapped to it;
centrifugal force flung the coin from his throat.
It poured projects: the gaz engine, the *atmospheric
    railway:*
trains, sucked uphill on leather sliding-valves.
    Pipe-dreams.

The tea clippers on the Avon were dressed rain-
    bow fashion.
Fanfares and gun salutes. *Foresight of reason*
stopped up its ears. A wee dark dot in a basket,
he whizzed along the cable over the chasm. A
    lonesome lemming, high up!
(The happy certainty of instinct.) A trip! A rush! A
    freak-out!

Metastases of the Empire, insurrections in India,
    Crimean and Opium wars,
mobile field hospitals for Florence Nightingale, the
    engineeress
of Charity. Each catastrophe a triumph. The admi-
    rals are *inept;*
I should like a contract to take Kronstadt.
I would found a Company to do it, and win!

The last venture—the adventure of the ships: each
    twice the size
of its predecessor. What had not been before be-
    came the norm. Cellular construction.
Propellers, cycloidal paddle-wheels, the crankshaft
forged in one piece, forty tons. Six times bigger
than anything that sailed the seas: the *Great East-*
    ern.

Half past noon. Up there, that's him, high on the
    platform.
He's bored. A flag signal, and the sledge-hammers
knock the wedges away from the cradle. The
    steam-winches howl,
the chains rattle, a sigh, a roll like an endless ruffle
    of drums,

a dull hacking in the iron hull, a shout, the earth
    trembles underfoot,

the ship gets underway. An Irish day-laborer
named O'Donovan, at the capstan, is caught in the
    crank, and crushed,
hurtled toward heaven. Odd how slowly the corpse
sails over the heads of the crowd! Hovering-like.
    Three thousand
curiosity-seekers, and no one notices. Then it starts
    raining.

Its original name was *Leviathan,* the monster.
    Hobbes,
or Job? After the launching came the carpenters,
    after the carpenters
the paper-hangers swarmed over the decks, and the
    landscape-painters.
Luxus necesse est: *All the geniuses of science on
    the wall paneling.*
And into the Grand Salon they rolled a rosewood
    grand piano.

His last penny went into the boat. Ruin, ruin! A
    redemption!
They hauled him out of a hatch the day of the
    maiden run,
paralyzed on one side. The final photo shows him
    in front of a hawse.
Giant iron links. He looks as if he were wearing
    widower's weeds.
Half Chaplin and half galley-slave: a top-hatted
    pessimist.

Many triumphs and catastrophes later, in the fall of
    '88,
when had one foot in oblivion, and *Nietzsche
    was setting out for Turino*
on his final journey, someone, in the scrap-metal of
    the *Great Eastern,*
stumbled upon two black skeletons, a riveter and
    his apprentice.
But historians, shrugging their shoulders, say: Old
    wives' tales.

C. R. D. (1809-1882)

The man who didn't want to.
The ground underfoot made him seasick.
"Epoch-making," "revolutionary," "brilliant," "a
    Titan,"
he didn't want to, he fought it
all the way, in every way,
with nausea, migraines, hypochondria.

School *simply a blank.*
He acted stupid. Out of mimicry, mediocre and
    lazy.
College, *repugnant, incredibly dull,*
a waste of time. No inkling of math,
forgot the classics, stayed *as ignorant as a pig*
about politicks, history, and moral philosophy.

They wanted him to be a doctor:
couldn't stand the sight of blood.
They tried to make a vicar out of him:
didn't know Latin.
A loser. Kept out of everything,
stayed put, avoided going all the way,
no push, no pull.

Marriage: *Grievous loss of time.*
Children: *Better than a dog anyhow.*
Shirked all fun.
Fun is the worst.

Then the famous world-voyage: half reluctantly,
half inadvertently. On board
he lay on the cardtable for hours,
giddiness, sluggishness.
Gathered samples, data, specimens.
Kept his convictions to himself.

One afternoon he read Malthus
(for amusement): palpitations,
violent shivers, and in his brain
an electric storm. From now on
he was lost. The rest was evolution:

The Origin of the Species originated
and developed, "naturally," irresistibly,
a new species of ideas, in a process
that crushes the crusher, slowly,
gradually, and relentlessly.

He retreated, married,
withdrew to an out-of-the-way hamlet,
avoided traveling, socializing,
shielded himself: *Pensioned at thirty-three.*

My mind seems to have become a kind of machine
for grinding general laws
out of large collections of facts.
Seven years on *The Structure and Distribution of*
        Coral Reefs.
Twenty-one years on *The Movements and Habits*
        of Climbing Plants.

Eight years on *A Monograph of the Cirripedia*
(two thick volumes describing all the living,
and two thin quartos the extinct species).

However, a solid structure forms from the shell,
protecting the body like an armour.
I therefore have nothing to record
during the rest of my life
except for the publication of my several books.

Daily schedule: at most four hours of work,
then the visit to the greenhouses.
A long siesta, wrapped in a cashmere
on the sofa. Change for dinner. After dinner
someone plays a piano sonata.

Early to bed. Insomnia:
His nights were usually bad,
he often lay awake or sat up in bed.

(Cf. fifteen miles away [as the crow flies]
another invalid, working reluctantly,
irresistibly, on revolution:
Liver ailments, nausea, furunculosis;
as worn as a fly, insomniac, plagued
by excess shitting of blood:
I am a machine, condemned
to devour books and then drop them
in a different form
on the dungheap of history.)

Endless details, accumulating like coral rag
in drawers, folders, registers.

Poor devil, his gardener remarked,
stands around staring
at a sunflower
for minutes on end.
If only he had something to do,
it would be a lot better for him.

A horrid languishing, a feeling
of fully withering.
Only science is left.
So much the worse.
Sometimes I hate it.

Didn't want to, never wanted to,
and yet all the way he doted on "Nature,"
with her gross waste, her base shoddiness,
and repugnant cruelty: methodically,
like a bookkeeper or an earthworm.

The Formation of Vegetable Mould
through the Action of Worms,
with Observations of their Habits.
The fruit of fifty years' work.
More significant in the history of the earth,
than one might think, they grind
the earth into humus in their gizzards,
tons of it, silently and irresistibly.

G. E. H. (1809-1891)

There were no bulldozers back then; so he used
    iron balls,
gigantic, chockfull of lead, swinging from scaf-
    folds, to smash
old Paris. *Artiste démolisseur*, pickax virtuoso, At-
    tila
of urban renewal, he even had the house he was
    born in
torn down. The future: big, bright, urgent.

The pleasure of destroying is also a creative plea-
    sure.
He smoked out the labyrinths of poverty (oh Baku-
    nin, that's
not what you meant!); one hundred thousand *rag-*
    pickers,
paupers, hookers, and crooks, had to escape con-
    struction
overhead and underfoot, outrageous rents, specula-
    tion.

His energy, endless; his gusto, gargantuan.
A bullish neck, a bearish build, broad shoulders.
    Get your foot in
before the bell rings! Off limits for beliefs.
Bureaucrat, go-getter, *pinworm on the state*
    shithead.
Rule by red tape: management is everything.

Silver braid, oakleaf on the blue coat, cocked hat
and sword. Boot-licking upwards: an *old roué* on
the throne.
(*The august hand has graciously issued an order.*)
Swaggering downwards:
A parvenu. Control and welfare hit it off: the
executive branch,
centralized like a factory, turned into technology.

With their measuring-rods and theodolites, the
surveyors deployed,
drew alignments, magistral lines: relentless perspectives.
Parliament: *a box of chatterboxes; legality no con-
sideration.*
Planning made room for cannon. The boulevards: *a
system*
of trenches against the mob lurking in the workers'
suburbs.

The City of Light is a job for specialists. Get en-
gineers,
stool-pigeons, bookkeepers, mapmakers. Empire
and empiricism.
He himself was incorruptible, i.e., he lived on his
expense account.
Private life: appropriate, stereotypical. He played
the market,
went to the usual balls, salons, soubrettes.

Fungating world-fairs. Patter-songs. The crowbar
spirit

spawned kitsch: Everything's new, everything's
    neo. Fashion
went flaunting under palms and draperies: remakes
    of remakes.
The ruins wreaked revenge as nostalgia. The scene
    of the crime
bared its wet concrete to the police in hissing gas-
    light.

Grandeur à la mooch, new jobs, deficit spending.
Miracles occurred of iron and glass, brokers gorged
    their guts,
graft went the rounds. The bears of high finance
shot up on credits. The ante doubled,
the boom zoomed, go for broke—the devil take the
    hindmost.

Undaunted, he put up monuments to himself: gas-
    works, graveyards, terminals,
law courts, cesspools, department stores, morgues,
    and outside the city
*the obelisks of industry, spewing their columns of
    smoke*
against the sky. The abattoirs majestic, the pissoirs
sporting the emperor's eagle: services beyond the
    call of duty:

No, foresight wasn't his thing. On old engravings,
the excavations gape like bomb craters. *(Since
    then,*
*with the big cities, how the means have grown to
    raze them to the ground:*

What images they conjure of things to come: Rotterdam,
Dresden, Hanoi.) A year after he resigned, Paris
burned.

F. C. (1810-1849)

A cheerful child: that much we know. Back then
    the castles
in the provinces were still all of wood. In the capi-
    tal,
the sidewalks weren't quite what they should be.
    The evenings
were still. Fire-sticks, hand-lanterns, torches.

They batten me as if I were a horse. Notwithstand-
    ing,
the Tsar gave him a diamond. Otherwise, little re-
    calls
those years: a couple of tickets, ribbons, pressed
    violets
under the glass of the vitrine, souvenirs of Warsaw.

The trip to the West was delayed. *My scores
are copied, my handkerchieves hemmed.* Paris
had cobblestones enough for four thousand bar-
    ricades.
The coaches were off schedule. It was a bloody
    year.

Yet the halls were sold out. Laurel wreaths, ban-
    quets. *All
that I have hitherto seen strikes me as unendura-
    bly out of date.*
Receptions at the Rothschilds and Radziwills. His
    touch discreet,
virtually waning: The hammers scarcely grazing
    the strings, said Berlioz.

The gas flames hissed on the Passage des
     Panoramas. There
two emigrés met. At the *Salon d'Automne,*
in the capital of the nineteenth century, a
     philosopher
from Berlin turned up. They talked about fashion.

     How grand
and poetic we are in our patent-leather shoes and
     cravats.
Is that a quote? Breakfast at the Café Anglais. Daut-
     remont frock-coats:
mauve. His linen—cambric. His complexion *almost*
     transparent.
Saying farewell, B. added: *The decisive strokes*

are executed with the left hand. But what are the
     decisive strokes?
The worshipping women: *educated magpies,*
     higher nobility. Any word about
his private life would be too much. *I am ill-fit for*
     concerts. The breath
of the, people stifles me. A meticulous worker.
     Legitimist. Dandy.

Distrusted all praise. Compared himself to a cy-
     press. *The piano*
is my alter ego. The critics saw "progress."
He acted chilly, sober, spoke about pure technique.
Yet he prescribed *voce sfogato* for the Barcarole:
     free and heedless.

The countesses said: *He coughs very gracefully.*
     This fatigue
was hard to account for. Baths in Enghien. Irritabil-
     ity.

Something deadly lodged in his larynx. The first
    hemmorrhage,
the February Revolution: *My concert had to be*
    canceled.

Instead, a trip to England. He played for the
    Queen.
The turf was pleasant, *but the stench of the coal!*
(Lack of commitment.) The economy of his works:
cannon sunken under flowers—sunken, or buried?

Do you have any pains, asked the doctor. (View of
    Place Vendôme.)
Answer: *No more.* He didn't possess
a bad conscience. His left hand was good.
The relentlessness with which he, throughout his
    life,

championed the most superfluous things is hard to
    explain.

M. A. B. (1814-1876)

There's only one thing I would wish, he cried, to
    keep my feeling
of revolt, which is sacred to me, keep it intact until
    the end.—
Barker, pig-headed, goddamn Kossack!—that is the
    love
for the phantastic, a chief defect in my char-
    acter.—Mohammed
without a Koran!—Relaxing will be the death of
    me.—A humbug,
A Pope, an ignoramus!—His heart and his head are
    made of fire.

Yes, Bakunin, that's how it must have been. Al-
    ways on the move,
crazy and unselfish. Unbearable, unreasonable, im-
    possible
all the time! For all I care, Bakunin, come back or
    stay where you are.

A long figure in a blue tailcoat on the Dresden bar-
    ricades,
with a countenance expressing the most brutal
    fury. Set fire
to the opera! And when all was lost, he demanded,
    pistol
in hand, that the Provisional Revolutionary Gov-
    ernment
be so kind as to blow itself (and him) up. (Curious
    sang-froid.)

The gentlemen rejected the motion by a large
    majority.

Do you remember, Bakunin? Always the same. Of
    course, you were a nuisance.
No wonder! And you're still one today. Under-
    stand? You're simply
a nuisance. And that's why I ask you, Bakunin: Come
    back.

Interrogated, shackled to the wall in the Olmütz
    casemates,
condemned to death, deported to Russia, *pardoned
    to perpetual imprisonment:*
a highly dangerous individual! A patron sent him
    a Lichtental
piano for his cell. He lost all his teeth.
For his opera *Prometheus* he invented *a sweet, la-
    menting melody,*
*rocking his leonine head to its beat in a childlike
    way.*

Ah, Bakunin, that's just like you. *(Rocking his
    leonine head:*
even twenty years later, in Locarno.) And because
    it's just like you,
and because you can't help us after all, Bakunin,
    stay where you are.

Sent to Siberia, and fleeing along the ice-blue
    Amur
over the Pacific, on steam sailers, sleighs, horses,
express trains, straight across the wilds of America,
    six months

nonstop, at last, in Paddington, right before New
    Year's,
leaping from the hansom, up the stairs, he threw
    himself
into Herzen's arms and shouted: *Where can I get
    some fresh oysters around here?*

Because you, in short, are inept, Bakunin, because
    you won't wash
as a decal a redeemer a bureaucrat a church father
a rightist or leftist cop—Bakunin: come back, come
    back.

Exile again. *Not just the rumble of rebellion, the
    clamor of the clubs,*
the tumult on the squares; but also the hectic eve,
*and the agreements, codes, and watchwords made
    him happy.*
A homeless celebrity, pursued by rumors, tall tales,
    and slander!
A magnetic heart, naive and extravagant! *He
    ranted and railed,*
*encouraged and derided, the livelong day and the
    livelong night.*

Didn't you? And because your *activity,* your *idle-
    ness,* your *appetite,*
your *perpetual perspiration* are *all but on a human
    scale,*
like you yourself, I therefore advise you, Bakunin,
    stay where you are.
His biographer, the all-knowing, says: He was im-
    potent. But Tatyana,

the little forbidden sister, playing the harp in the
    white manor-house,
drove him wild. True, his three children weren't
    his.
But to Netchayev, the mythomaniac, the murderer,
    the Jesuit, blackmailer.
and martyr of the Revolution, he wrote: *My little
    tiger, my boy,*
*my wild darling! (The despotism of the illuminati
    is the worst.)*

Oh well, let's forget about love, Bakunin. You
    didn't want to die.
You were no politico-economic angel of death.
    Muddled
like us, and artless. Come back, Bakunin! Bakunin,
    come back.

At last the night in Bologna. It was August. He
    stood at the window.
He listened. Nothing stirred in the town. The
    tower-clocks struck.
The insurrection was wrecked. Dawn was coming.
    He hid
in a hay-wagon. His beard shaved off, in a cleric's
    habit,
a basket of eggs on his arm, green spectacles, he
    hobbled on his stick
to the station, to die in Switzerland, in bed.
That was a long, long time ago. Most likely too
    early, as usual,

or too late. Nothing disproved you, you proved
    nothing,
and therefore stay, stay where you are, or, for all I
    care, come back.

Enormous masses of flesh and fat, dropsy, bladder
    complaints.
A ranting laughter, he chain-smoked, gasped, driv-
    en by asthma.
he read encoded telegrams and wrote in sympathe-
    tic ink:
Exploting and governing: one and the same. He
    was bloated and toothless.
Everything covered with tobacco ashes, teaspoons,
    newspapers. The police agents
ambling in front of the house. Chaos and filth all
    over. Time running out.

Europe still reeks of police. Therefore, and because
    never and nowhere,
Bakunin, has there ever been, will there ever be, a
    Bakunin monument,
Bakunin, I ask you: come back, come back, come
    back.

I. P. S. (1818-1865)

All his words and deeds exuded
unending loving kindness.
The Vienna Maternity Hospital
was the world's biggest. *Splendid,*
this opportunity of dissecting
the fresh female corpses
in the death-chamber every morning.
He performed these peculiar examinations
with extraordinary perserverance.
He was fairly bald, *of a childishly*
naive mentality, and somewhat obese.

The mortality, between eighteen
and thirty-six percent,
made an indelible impression
on his mind. But at masked balls,
the Csárdás burnt like a frenzy.
He danced for joy, and three times
an evening he changed (that's how feverish
he felt) his linen. Only later
was he afflicted by those
sorrowful stirrings *that make life*
all but enviable.

Opinions of leading clinicians
on the origins of childbed fever
(a selection): *Blood crases; swamp air;*
injurious effects of a dead foetus;
miasmas; also a lack of ventilators;

nearby mortuary chambers and cesspools;
retained milk, certain influences
of a cosmic and tellurian nature.
In short, superstitious mumbo-jumbo.
Everything unexplained, everything doubtful,
but not the enormous number of corpses.

An introvert, provisional assistant
from the provinces. Rather shy. Yet to all
the medical faculties in the world
I say: You teach error!
It's the pestilential air, it's
the necrotic poison, the putrid,
gangrenous, wet ulcer, that's what,
the decaying parts of bodies,
the foul matter, the sponges,
the linen, the spoons, the scissors,
the bedpans and the blades of the forceps;

it's the lubricated finger, the inner,
cadaverous, touching hand, yes,
it's the doctor's hand that kills!
All you need is one single ounce
of chloride of lime,
only one ounce per pail of water,
to put an end to the poisoning.
He often gazed at his strikingly
pudgy and skillful hands,
burst into tears and, no longer
in control of himself, was forced
to break off the lecture.

Commissions convened,
found nothing. Someone laughed.
The prevailing academic opinion prevailed.
In the wards, the women died on.
The weapons of Mafiosi were septic:
the oily report and the dry rescript,
the doctored statistics, the dull,
paralyzing silence. *You, Herr Court Councilor,
are an accomplice to this massacre!*
Thus, utterly enraged by the hostilities
confronting him, he wrote

wild, abusive, unwieldy things,
digressing, repeating himself,
going in circles: *The murdering*
he wrote, *must stop,*
and to make the murdering stop,
I shall keep watch. *Murderers,*
he wrote *(To All Obstretricians!)*
are what I call all who
transgress my rules,
for they act as criminals.
He saw agents everywhere, phantoms.

His friends didn't recognize him.
He grew fat from heartache, looked
distorted. *(A* phantom, *in medical parlance,*
refers to a leather-covered
artificial or natural
female pelvis [true and false],
employed in teaching
the technique of operations.)

On the streets of Budapest
he put up posters:
I warn you against the physicians!

A childish nature, peculiarities:
Walked around in his room undressed
and absently put his feet up on the table.
*in all of which things his derangement
could no longer be denied.*
Behind him in the corridor—
giggling. *Thus men must for all time
reckon him among the greatest
benefactors of humanity and always
lament the dismal lot
that befell him.*

It's two in the afternoon.
A mob of enemies are after him.
He sees them clearly, as black
as flies, in their prince alberts,
and he flees into the
anatomical theater.
On the marble block, a body.
He seizes the scalpel, cuts
open the corpse, throws flesh around,
burrows in the bowels, threatens,
cuts himself, they disarm him,
he dies after three weeks of agony.

But that's not how it was. Those are dreams,
exaggerations! In reality,
it was a peaceful and beautiful

Sunday in July, and he went along
of his own free will. He didn't
put up a fight until evening.
*Six attendants scarcely sufficed
to subdue him.* Straitjacket,
dark room. The septic wound
on his middle finger was noticed too late.
Blood poisoning: *Thus he did not live
to witness the triumph of his theory.*

E. J. M. (1830-1904)

His drug was facts. Always proper,
a wine-dealer's son from the Côte d'Or, portly,
a positivist in a square collar and a pince-nez,
buttoned-up behind his apparatus,
he lay in wait, immobile, for any motion, hunted
the fleeing quarry: *the very language*
of phenomena, a phantom. On Rue
de l'Ancienne Comédie, a new spectacle was
    mounted.

The professor rented a stage, auditorium,
    dressing-rooms.
Partitions, hastily put up: the small parlor
with the piano, the mechanical workshop, and
(to be reached by breakneck stairs) a study,
a bed, an archive. What was left was an enormous
    room,
the ring, waxed to a shine, in which,
before black and white cloths, on swings,
on strings, in lamplight, the facts revealed them-
    selves.

The pigeon, tied to the jib of a merry-go-round—
does it fly, or is it flown? The trail
of its wings is invisible: yet it's followed by,
pneumatically steering through a chaos
of tubes and drums, a steel spike;
quivering, it scratches the soot-blackened paper.
What writes and draws there, measuring itself,
is a hallucination, known as "Nature."

Patterns of mathematical elegance, relationships
between frequency and tonus, temperature
and pressure: undulations, oscillations, leaps.
All variables of locomotion: *La machine animale.*
In air and in water. The eel, the pianist,
the mollusk, the salamander's heart: the tractrix,
the cissoid: curves (banking, intersecting, envelop-
    ing),
vortices, trajectories, diagrams. . . . In short, "the
    world"

is an optical illusion: We see nothing
"as it is," whatever reveals itself, conceals itself.
Ever subtler snares, more clever instruments.
ever more abstract weapons. The physiologist aims
with the photographic *rapid-fire gun:*
the shutter opens sixteen times a minute,
and the white seagull in front of the black curtain
leaves *an infinitely radiant image* behind.

He tinkered, designed, built the first movie camera
in the world. Not to film: he wanted to see.
On the Champs-Élysées, a man gets off
his bicycle; no one knows how.
Only slow-motion shows all. So he invented it.
His theater filled up with astrophysicists, physi-
    cians,
the shining lights of science. (Way in the back,
there sat, unnoticed, a certain Edison, capitalist.)

To study an insect, I have to construct insects.
So the researcher became a demiurge: he counter-
    feited

abstract hearts, propeller-driven birds,
machines that could breathe. It crept across the waxed
parquet: the facsimile of a snake. He cast in bronze:
the seagull's flight. A fantastic creature:
four-dimensional fluttering, curdled locomotion,
flowing stasis. Time we can touch.

A fool whose hand turned anything into an artifact,
idolater of the science of exploitation,
innocent lamb who blazed a trail for Taylor's terror,
unwitting forebear of Hollywood, an artist
on the side, an inventor willy-nilly, Mallarmé
by mistake, a genius of reproduction: Motionless,
the eye of the Great Observer gazes at us,
matt-violet, a blind iris of silver bromide.

H. M. S. (1841-1904)

Picture postcard   (1)
False consciousness in a pith helmet.
Heroism, hand-painted.
Jungles, deserts, prairies: nothing but backdrops.
Every gesture posed, history
a pretext for scoops.
To be continued.
Hack, idealist, mercenary,
expense-account spender, go-getter, agent,
Tourist of blood-baths,
blow-fly of genocide:
Quelling the Kiowa, Comanche, and Sioux (1867),
expedition against Abyssinia (1868),
massacre on the Gold Coast (1873):
always there *in his high-minded way.*

Inventory of an Expedition   (1)
A leader, an adjutant, an assistant adjutant, a
rifle-bearer, an interpreter, a staff sergeant, three
sergeants, 23 guards, 157 porters, a cook, a tailor, a
carpenter, two horses, 27 donkeys, a dog, a few
goats;
    71 crates of ammunition, candles, soap, coffee,
tea, sugar, flour, rice, sardines, pemmican, Dr.
Liebig's extract of meat, pans, pots, three tents, two
collapsed boats, a bath.

Picture postcard   (2)
A higher mission: *To raise the degenerate*

members of the family of man
to our level (Livingstone).
Spoiled children, troglodytes,
infernal riffraff: thievish, trusting,
superstitious, cruel, good-natured, stupid,
unreliable, cowardly, blood-thirsty, shiftless.
Kalulu, my Prince, my King, my slave:
the boy, worshipped and whipped.
The weals on that small, despised,
adorable, unreachable black bottom.
Chaste, unspoiled Nature.
The Dark Continent:
Discover, explore, penetrate.
Punishments *for my wicked self:*
insects, lianas, underbrush,
mud, tropical rain, toads,
icy fog, morass, thirst, fever,
sores, blazing sun, hunger,
strange diseases, traps,
poisoned arrows, cataleptic trances,
suicidal thoughts, madness.

Inventory of an Expedition   (2)
Ten miles of unbleached American calico; five
miles of Indian twill, blue, lightweight; three miles
of pink muslin and crimson broadcloth;

   beads: 36,500 necklaces of a million beads,
eleven different colors and sorts, made of glass,
china or coral; sizes 5 (marbles) to 0 (seed-pearl);
black, brick, dove-grey, coral pink, and palm-green;

   350 lbs of no. 5 and no. 6 gauge brass-wire in
the normal spools.

Picture postcard (3)
A single private man
added over three million
square miles
to the civilized world.
Comité d'Études du Haut-Congo.
Branch-lines, docks,
rare wood, rubber, and ivory:
Suffer the little children to come unto me!
The grand hall of the Brussels stock exchange,
decorated with African spears,
at the center a tropical bouquet,
with four hundred elephant's tusks sprouting out.
Red kepis for the chieftains,
the cast-off liveries of the lackeys.
Radiant light of Christianity.

Inventory of an Expedition (3)
Two sixteen shooters (one Winchester, one Henry);
three single-shot breechloaders (two Starrs, one
Jocelyn); one elephant gun; one double-barreled
breechloading smooth-bore gun; two revolvers, 24
flintlock muskets, six pistols, a battle-ax, two
swords, two Persian daggers, one boar-spear, 26
hatchets, and 24 butcher's knives.

Picture postcard (4)
Timid, weepy, always offended:
I was not born into this world
to be happy. Big feet,
red face. Malaria for 25 years:
The shivers. The bed quivered,

the glasses on the night table
jingled all night. Senility.
Bought himself a tiny estate in Surrey.
The garden a Lilliput Africa, a Kraal
on the stone building-blocks.
Raked gravel paths through the Arumini Jungle,
a gooseberry bed; a path led across the Congo:
Forget-me-not. *And my thoughts*
roared like the mighty organ
in the Crystal Palace.

Envoi
Stuffed by his own hand,
a mummy of papier-mâché.
A slight smell of mothballs
surrounds the trophy in the Tropical Museum.
The stench of the corpses
he left behind
is scarcely perceptible.

F. W. T. (1856-1915)

Only a lunatic can keep that busy. *Yes, Mama.*
    Conscientiously
filling the sugar bowls, brushing himself off, play-
    ing the piano,
taking his cold bath on schedule, scraping his
    plate,
and he mowed the lawn beneath the magnolia
    trees terribly often.

Drenched with sweat, he jumped out of his sleep.
    So at thirteen
he sewed himself a leather harness, spiked his bed
    with wooden nails.
The dreamer, upon rolling over on his back, in-
    stantly
pricked himself awake before fear could catch him
    red-handed.

A shackled man. *The word I never pops up in his*
    writings.
Teetotaler, nonsmoker, no coffee or tea. *A life*
fully dedicated to the welfare of the working-man.
    Yes, Mama.
The name of the first steel monopoly was
    Bethlehem. Get tougher.

Work harder and save! No flunky was ever gutsier,
Piecework rat race against shiftlessness. *Let's be*
    friends.

(Labor and Capital!) It's really depressing to think
they never killed him, that fakir, who hollered at
    them:

You are not supposed to think! Up the norm, get
    the stopwatch.
Split the working class with every flick of the
    wrist, mangle it. Vivisection,
absolute subordination of the masses. (Lenin ad-
    mires him.)
Our bed of nails is production. The prophet
    preaches

the science of steel-cutting, the science of belting,
the sciences of brick-laying, of brushing,
and piano-playing, logically exploited to the ut-
    most degree,
and the science of the mortification of all flesh.
    Yes, there they are:

The next goals of Soviet power: the best surveil-
    lance systems,
the grandest achievements! Yes, Mama. *At home,*
on the farm, in every church, in all government
    agencies.
The exploitation of science becomes the science of
    exploitation.

Always *healthy and normal:* Misshapen, he dozes
    while sitting,
sleepless against misshapen pillow-strongholds. A
    social automaton.

Impotent all his life. Yes, Mama. A yellowed photo
        shows a beefy man
with droopy eyelids, in a rosy blouse and a frilly
        coat.

Otherwise: steam hammers, a hundred patents. The
        best cutting-angle
for flat-nosed fast-spinning scrubbing-steel.
        Maximum prosperity
must be top priority for everyone. He lived very
        privately,
grew roses, and, when dying, he painstakingly
        wound his pocket-watch.

The curtain goes up. He claps his hands. The stage
    is blank.
Robert-Houdin's been dead for ages. In the
    quarter-trap
on the Passage de l'Opéra, the dust drifts from the
    magic machines.
The Undrainable Bottle's been killed. *The Omnis-*
cient Bat's gone silent.
Paris leaves *The Phantastic Illusions* yawning. *The*
Skull Surgeon
is booed and hissed. *The Astronomer's Dream* is
    no longer a draw.
The Decapitated Head falls flat. The show-booth
    has dark nights.
The Master staggers, has an idea.

He claps his hands. A glass pavilion unfolds in
    Montreuil
as though by a ghostly hand. A palmery. A
    menagerie.
Arc lamps pop up from the parquet. Blocks and
    tackles rise aloft.
Blinds roll up and down. Tin chests and cranks
    and lenses
move on trestles and tripods. Cloths wave. Trap-
    doors drop.
An entire studio sprouts and spreads with dark-
    rooms,

decors, models, scenery, costumes: a miracle-
    making theater-machinery,
a ghost-manufacturing factory.

Your trade and mine—not much difference, says
    Apollinaire.
The Master hews and screws and writes. He paints
    and films.
He cuts and tailors. He fashions. He builds. He de-
    velops.
He hammers and mixes and copies and does every-
    thing himself and answers: *I*
work with both my head and my hands. He plays
    seven musicians,
an entire orchestra at once. He claps his hands.
The screen goes dark. The celluloid jerks and jolts.
He's the first, always the first.

The camera whirrs. A car appears and stalls and
    turns
into a hearse. Four white clowns turn into a giant
    Negro.
At a furious pace, everything turns into everything
    else. Then bursts.
Then blasts into a thousand pieces. The film is
    over. The flick begins.
The Songs of Maldoror flicker across the white
    wall. Scholars ambulate
on the ceiling. Clocks spew demons out. An opium
    fiend dreams.
Ladies spring forth from umbrellas. Gulliver wanes
    and waxes.
The first commercial cuts Burnibus mustard.

A coffer coughed up by a coffer coughs up count-
    less coffers.
All disasters of progress whiz past as a nightmare,
    as slapstick,
as fairyland. The Master claps his hands. The
    lights go on.
He invented everything. The freeze-frame. The
    fade. The scenario. Double exposure. Single-
    frame animation. The lap dissolve. The
    studio.
The sea of his inventions crashes in upon him,
    phosphorescingly
black and white. Hand-colored girls color the
    image with tiny brushes.
It ran, the very first color film.

He claps his hands. He imitates epochs.
The Explosion of the Battleship Maine at Havana.
    The Dreyfus Trial.
The Eruption of Mont Pelé and *The Coronation of*
    Edward VII of England.
The producer hunts history down in the studio. It's
    all so much Better,
Finer, Sharper, and Realer than in reality! A demi-
    urge, they're saying,
a magus, *an alchemist of light!* Okay by me. But he
    doesn't look it.
With that vandyke, embonpoint, and moustachio,
    bald and jovial, he's more
like a flea-circus owner.

He claps his hands. The entire theater collapses.
The films burn up. The machines turn to scrap by

themselves. Wrack and ruin.

The decorations hop to the dump. A soot-slide buries the inventor.

A steamroller leaves him flat on the asphalt. How tragic. Then years pass.

In a kiosk at Gare Montparnasse, there sits a very old man.

He sells toys, candy, and tiny trumpets. He claps his hands.

No one recalls. Nothing happens. That was his last stunt.

Now you see him, now you don't.

U. C. (1877-1963)

I

And *I proceeded to the slaughter-house* (and was Director of the Neurobiological Institute of Milan) and *I saw the skulls of the hogs between the heavy metal tongs* (and my study on Via Savoia) *and the switch* (and my antique bronze statuettes on the desk) and *I noticed the way the animals sank down unconscious and stiffened* (and Professor of Neuropsychiatry at the universities of Bari Genoa Rome) and *the way they were overcome by convulsions within a few seconds* (and inventor of a time-fuse for artillery and airforce) and *I felt that there was extremely valuable material here for my experiments* (and my decorations and gold medals) and *I decided to determine what duration what voltage and what method would be required for bringing about the death of the hogs* (and President of the Italian Society of Psychiatry) and *I sent electric currents through their skulls from different sides* (and honorary member of the Committee of Biology and Medicine of the National Research Board) *and through their trunks for several minutes* (and nominee for the Nobel Prize) and *it struck me that the animals seldom were killed when the current flowed through their heads* (and my housekeeper and my smoke dispeller in the guise of a porcelain owl) *and that they remained prostrate for a number of minutes after a violent cataleptic fit* (and an honorary doctorate from the

Sorbonne, Paris) *and that they raised themselves up again with great difficulty* (and honorary doctorates from the universities of Rio de Janeiro and Saõ Paolo and Montreal for pioneering studies on goiters and cretinism) *and that they tried to flee*

II

And *I directed my assistants to be on the look-out for a suitable subject* (and VV *Il Duce*) and on 4/15/1938 the Police Commissioner of Rome committed a person to me for observation (and *Fascism climbed over the decaying body of the goddess of Freedom)* and *I quote from his accompanying letter* (and Italians! Black Shirts! Legioneers!) "S. E., engineer and 39 years old and picked up at the Railroad Terminal and without a ticket and evidently not in full possession of his mental faculties" (and unending ovations) and *I selected this man for my first experiment on a human being*

III

And *I placed two electrodes on his temples* (and the most important indications are schizophrenia and paranoia) *and I decided to begin with 80 volts alternating current and 0.2 seconds* (and alcoholism and drug addiction and depressions and melancholy) and *his muscles became rigid* (and the most important side-effects are loss of memory and nausea and panic) and *he reared up* (and that is the typical position called the jumping-jack position by Von Braunmühl et al.) *and he collapsed but without loss of consciousness* (and the most important complications are fractures of the legs, arms, jaw, and spine) *and he began singing very loudly* (and heart trouble and internal bleeding) *and then he grew still and did not move*

IV

And naturally this meant a great emotional strain for me (and according to Reil [1803] noninjurious torture is a *dictate in medicine*) *and I consulted with my assistants about inserting a pause* (and according to Squire [1937] the length of the amnesia is not known) *and the man was listening to us and suddenly he said in a loud, solemn voice: "Don't do it again. You'll kill me."* (and according to Sogliano [1943] the treatment *can be repeated with no misgivings up to five times within ten minutes*) *and I confess that my heart sank* (and according to Kalinowski et al. [1946], *straps and fetters are to be kept in readiness in case the patient becomes dangerous and violent*) *and I had to pull myself together to keep from yielding to this superstitious* sentiment (and according to Sakel et al. [1965], *there is unfortunately no scientific basis so far for electro-shock*) *and I took hold of myself and gave him another charge of 110 volts*

V

And ever since, in the closed wards, in their pajamas, they climb up on the white-enameled iron beds *(and we shall never forget his pioneering deed)* and they get an injection and in case of resistance another injection *(and his achievements in scientific progress)* and four orderlies hold them down on their hands and feet *(and his prolific work)*

and stuff a rubber tube in their mouths and adjust
the cold chromium plates on their temples (and *his
unquenchable thirst for knowledge*) and in the
slaughteryards you hear no more bellowing and
mooing and bleating (and *his genuine humanism*)
and then the boss gives them the juice (and *unfortunately there is no scientific basis for it so far*)
and then they're out and then they come to and
then they're snuffed

V. M. M. (1890-   )

Heavily breathing, under the blossoming apple
    tree,
behind the dacha, Vyacheslav Mikhailovich
slides around on his wicker chair,
the survivor. Pensioned, pensioned, pensioned.

His Iron Ass, it ain't what it
used to be. Only the pencil-sharpener
on his watch-chain recalls the sunny years
in the politbureau. He broods, cracks his knuckles.

Insignificant as a Bolshevik: the group of
    "Chemists."
I myself was in prison! (Justifications.)
Ready for rebellion, for death. Surrounded by
    souvenirs.
Why, the facts are nothing but propaganda.

E.g., way back when, in the *Reich* Chancellery, the
    November rain
whipped the windows. *The friendship between us
is cemented with blood.* Did he really say that?
Dinner-speeches editorials memos: History?

A history? Who can tell!?
Who can remember?! The flies buzz
in back rooms and cells. The record reads:
Scum. Mad dogs. Dangerous swine.

His own wife, deported like all the others.
Her eyes, were they green or brown? And the kids?
Insignificant: What does that signify? *Milksop!*
screamed Lenin. A mummy sits in the cottage.

The flies buzz as usual. Survived, surviving.
Falling asleep, falling awake. In his dreams
he confuses homework and death verdicts.
He was always a good student. Only his English

got rusty. *Cocktail* for instance: a foreign word,
unintelligible. Hard of hearing: no blasts
burst in his ears. Cracking knuckles.
He listens. Is that the flies? Drawling,

the thin etudes return, *Rêverie, Un sospiro,*
which he played way back when in Kukarski,
district of Nolinsk, in the year nineteen hundred
        and three,
expressive, and inspired with lofty feelings.

W. R. (1897-1957)

That summer of '37 he was supposedly almost
    happy.
White nights, boats on the Oslo Fjord, or with
    Sigurd
and Nic and Arnulf in the *Teater Café*, with the
    golden aquavit:
the violinist played Ravel's *Bolero*, the patrons
    whispered:

That's him! Naturally they were right, naturally
he was crazy, a cripple, who hit out on all sides,
routed all his friends: Confessions, in black and
    white
(Oh shades of Stalin), wrung from them (those
    traitors),

and he locked the slips in the desk. (Yes, one also
calls that paranoia.) *You'll understand me in a
    thousand years.*
Just what does that mean: a rebel? He would rather
    have sat
among the mirthful. Like a child catching a mos-
    quito,

and listening to his clenched fist: What he held in
    his hand
pulsated and seemed alive. *It* writhed. Id. But no
    one
would believe him. Get evidence, then! Geiger
    counters,

stopwatches, microscopes. The *Faraday of the or-
    gasm,*

a guru, a dilettante, and these were his findings:
It is love that works everything, it is measurable,
its color is blue, it moves the stars, the frogs,
the clouds. (That roaring in the boy's skull never
    left him.)

An estate in Bukovina. A potato fire, dusty high-
    ways,
the throbbing of the thresher. Bedroom secrets in
    the manor,
a suicide at the carp pond, and later, lifelong,
the itching under the skin, the eczema of memory.)

He loved the green uniform, the Austro-Hungarian
    braids and spurs,
loved carnations, diplomas, honors, his white
    smock,
dreamt of riding in triumph through the Branden-
    burg Gate,
on a white stallion, to the peal of Ravel's clarinets.

Under the banner of Marxism: yellowed notebooks.
    Seriously,
he fought against oppression, helped many people,
yet when his daughter, aged two, sang *Oh Christ-
    mas Tree,*
there was a hail of slaps, and he intoned the *Inter-
    nationale.*

Next, only gibberish, science fiction. Life vescicles
against the *emotional plague*. Vegeto-bio-orgone-
    energetics, in short:
The orgasm is the orgasm is the orgasm.
Women will remain cooks, secretaries, guinea pigs.

Celluloid on the outside, glass wool on the inside,
    iron turnings,
airholes in the top. The accumulator gathers the
    wonder energy,
the rays of salvation. Excitedly the girls settled
    down,
and the disciples, in the upright coffin. The exper-
    iment began.

The pulse beat faster, the thermometer rose: a
    proof!
He hung signs up everywhere: *It can be done!* The
    love rays
drive engines, bring rain, and heal everything:
    cancer,
schizophrenia, the traces of the hydrogen
    bomb. . . .

But then the mice up and died in the basement,
    with reddened eyes
the disciples crept out of their boxes, blinked,
    threw up,
everything's somehow gone wrong, and when he
    got excited,
his eczema broke out, he drank too much, he
    smoked,

he coughed, shaken by heart attacks, his inventions
were taken away from him, the women cheated
    him, he was scared
of fires, spies, storms, and kidnappers.
People laughed at him, killed him with silence.
    Whose fault?

It was the mafia of scholars, it was the hounding
    (quack,
Jewish pornographer), it was the Bolsheviks, agents
were swarming everywhere, a conspiracy this, his
    home
might be searched, the books were burnt: Blackout.

From the cosmos, the enemy came with flying sau-
    cers,
their exhausts blackened rocks, poisoned every-
    thing. TOP SECRET!
Drivel. If he didn't act with his miracle
    weapons. . . .
The First Battle for the Universe. . . . He, the Dis-
    coverer,

led here in handcuffs, refused to give any informa-
    tion.
His defense was confused, he slackened, he lapsed
    into silence.
Oh Dr. Mabuse! Oh Maniac of Redemption! Oh
    Rosicrucian of Fucking!
Oh Junkman of Science! Oh Ventriloquist of Christ!

Oh helpless helper of humanity! Oh mystical
     technocrat!
Oh cabalist from a horror flick! Oh broken
     liberator!
The bombers circled over the prison, false, dread-
     ful,
the clarinets played off-key at the grave, it was all
     for nothing.

A. M. T. (1912-1954)

It's certain that he never read a newspaper; that he knitted his gloves himself; that he always kept losing trunks, books, coats; and that, whenever he broke his stubborn silence at meals, he fell into *a shrill stuttering* or *a cackling laugh*. His eyes were a radiant, inorganic blue, *like stained glass*.

Very well then. Let us imagine a universal automaton A, which is capable of simulating any other automaton. A_n. A is a black box fed with an endless strip of paper; this band is the outer world of the machine. It is divided into fields, each single one of which is either blank or marked. We now imagine that A patiently reads one field after another, moving the strip one field forward or backward, and/or writes a mark and/or erases a mark, and we name this apparatus, after its inventor, a Turing machine.

We know moreover that he carefully isolated himself; that he wore rags, sailed in steerage, slept in flea-bags. Evidently he was out to delete himself. One night in his villa, a broken-down house, he inadvertently, as in an Agatha Christie novel, poisoned himself with cyanide. Any similarity with persons living or dead is purely coincidental.

Furthermore we may state that every special automaton, whether calculating satellite orbits, writing mazurkas, or producing other automatons, is merely a state A_n of A. This holds even for the case that A_n is twice as large or many times as complicated as A.

He cut his own gears, on a lathe in his potato cellar. *Fed up with public transportation he would walk for miles* overland. He could fix radios and other devices with string. The secret service appreciated him because he could break any code. However, he readily fainted, even for no apparent reason.

We realize that it is impossible to predict fully what solutions the automaton can or cannot provide. In every closed and sufficiently extensive system there are indeterminable propositions. It may sound funny, but the fact is that the proof can only be supplied by the proof. In addition, we must establish that the universal automaton is infinitely indolent, and that it has never been constructed.

Aside from that, he used to bike through the rain; whereby he found it practical to strap an alarm clock to his belt and to put on a gas mask; the former, in order to be always punctual, the latter to coddle his hayfever, for he suffered from asthma; nevertheless, this is a human trait that puts our minds at ease. We do not know why he always avoided contact with the skin of other people of either sex.

In regard to the Turing machine, however, we propose an experiment. One of us, let us call him B, takes up contact with it (by means of a data processing machine or a teletype). C, a censor, is to supervise the dialogue. A simulates a human being, and so does B; and now C must decide which of the two is the human being and which the machine. Let us call this experiment a Turing game, after its inventor.

One can invent masterpieces in the art of automata without even building or working a single machine, just as one can devise methods for reckoning the movements of a star that one has never laid eyes on. (Condorcet)

Whenever the machine betrays itself (either by making or, on the contrary, by not making, a mistake), it improves its program. It learns and learns. This raises the question as to when the match will end. We do not answer this question, but we do maintain that the game can last for a very long time and that it has never been played.

At any rate, there is no quelling the rumor that sometimes, especially on damp October days, in the environs of Cambridge, one can see him, or his simulacrum, on mowed stubblefields, hiking in the fog across country, unpredictably doubling back.

E. G. de la S. (1928-1967)

For a while thousands wore his little beret on their
    heads,
and thousands and thousands more carried big pic-
    tures
of his picture and hollered his name out very loud.
Those processesions downtown now seem
as unreal as the country and class he was born in.

Far from the slaughterhouses and barracks and
    brothels,
his father's villa crumbled on the river. The money
    evaporated,
but the swimming pool was maintained. A shy
    child,
allergic, often close to choking to death. Battled
    with his body,
smoked cigars, became (whatever that means) a
    man.

Jules Verne lay under his pillow. His first attack,
his first flight into reality: *Tristes Tropiques*.
But the lepers under the rotting veranda on the
    Amazon
didn't understand what he said, and kept dying.
    Only then
did he find the foe to whom he stayed loyal all his
    life,

and the foe of the foe. Just a few victories later,
the New Man appeared to him, an old idea, very
   new.
But economy didn't listen to his speeches. There
   was no spaghetti.
Nor any toothpaste, and what is toothpaste made
   from?
The banknotes he signed were worthless.

The sugar stuck to shirts. Machines, paid for with
   hard currency,
decayed on quais. La Rampa rumbled with rumors.
Bowing and scraping in Moscow, new credits. The
   people lined up,
were unreliable, cracked hungry jokes. Agents everywhere,
intrigues he never understood. A foreigner forever.

Tried to moralize to the Russians. The lover of
   humanity
yelled for the *hatred which shall transform hu-*
   manity into
a violent, effective, cold killing-machine. Actually
a mimosa: his favorite pastime, reading poems. (He
   knew
Baudelaire inside out.) A tender failure, food for
   secret services.

So he fled to the weapons, remaining there, where
   all was clear
and lucid: foe foe and treason treason, in the
   jungle.
But he himself seemed extinguished. *Round,*
   beardless, graying temples,

thick glasses, like a salesman, a duffle coat, in this
fancy dress in Ñancahuazú he went about his final
    work.

Spoke no Quechua, no Guaraní. *The silence of the
    Indians*
*was absolute, as though we came from another
    world.* Insects,
lianas, underbrush. *The peasants like rocks.* Colics,
coughing fits, edemas. Overdoses of cortisone.
    Adrenalin.
Gasping till the last injection: *Ave Maria purisima!*

*The legend was spreading like foam. We're already
supermen, invincible. (Always that deadly irony,*
unnoticed by his comrades.) *A human wreck, an
    idol.*
We would have hired him, the most progressive
of his enemies advertised. Instead they displayed
    his corpse

with hands cut off. *A mystical adventure,* and
*a passion irresistibly reminiscent of the image of
    Christ:*
that's what his followers wrote. He: *Les honneurs,
    ça m'emmerde.*
It's not that long ago, and forgotten. Only the histo-
    rians
settle in like the moths in the cloth of his uniform.

Holes in the popular war. Otherwise, in Met-
    ropolis, only
a boutique that stole his name speaks of him.
On Kensington High Street, the incense sticks are

glowing;
next to the cash register, the last hippies sit sullen,
unreal, like fossils, and unquestioning, and almost
    immortal.

The text breaks off, and calmly the answers keep
    ganging up.

Index

BLANQUI, Louis Auguste, *French politician*
(1805-1881) *78*

Bochard de Saron, Jean Baptiste, *French
astronomer* (1730-1794) *48,49*

Boole, George, *Anglo-Irish mathematician*
(1815-1864) *26*

Borgia, Cesare, *duke of Valentinois and
Romagna* (1475-1507) *7*

Boussingault, Jean Baptiste, *French chemist*
(1802-1887) *64*

BRAHE, Tyge, *Danish astronomer*
(1546-1601) *14*

BRUNEL, Isambard Kingdom, *English
engineer* (1806-1859) *64,86*

Brunel, Sir Marc Isambard, *English engineer*
(1769-1849) *87*

Büchner, Georg, *German writer* (1813-1837)
75

Byron, George Gordon Noel Lord, *Scottish
poet* (1788-1824) *76*

C. B., *see* Babbage

C.F., *see* Fourier

C. M., *see* Messier

C. R. D., *see* Darwin

C. von L., *see* Linné

CAMPANELLA, Tommaso, *Italian philosopher*
(1568-1639) *18*

Céline, Louis Ferdinand, *French novelist*
(1894-1961) *111*

CERLETTI, Ugo, *Italian psychiatrist*
(1877-1963) *127*

Chaplin, Charlie, *English movie actor*
(1889-   ) *90*

CHOPIN, Frédéric, *Polish composer*
(1810-1849) *88,100*

Christian IV, *King of Denmark* (1577-1648)
16

Christie, Agatha, *English writer* (1890-1976)
138

Columbus, Christopher, *Italian navigator*
(1443-1506) *68*

CONDORCET, Antoine Caritat Marquis de,
French philosopher and mathematician
(1743-1794) *53,59,140*

DARWIN, Charles Robert, *English biologist*
(1809-1882) *92*

Dautremont, *Parisian tailor* (active c.
1830-1850) *101*

Debray, Régis, *French journalist* (1940-   )
143

Delisle, Joseph, *French astronomer*
(1688-1768) *47*

Descartes, René, *French philosopher*
(1596-1650) *20,68*

Diderot, Denis, *French writer and
philosopher* (1713-1784) *33*

DONDI, Giovanni de', *Italian clockmaker*
(1318-1389) *1,3*

Dreyfus, Alfred, *French officer* (1859-1935)
125

E. G. de la S., *see* Guevara

E. J. M., *see* Marey

Edison, Thomas Alva, *American inventor
and entrepreneur* (1847-1931) *114*

Edward VII, *king of England* (1841-1910)
125

Emerson, Ralph Waldo, *American writer*
	(1803-1882) *74*
Engels, Friedrich, *German social scientist*
	(1820-1895) *59,65,80,81,87,103*
EVANS, Oliver, *American inventor*
	(1755-1819) *56*
F. C., *see* Chopin
F. W. T., *see* Taylor
Faraday, Michael, *English physicist and*
	chemist (1791-1867) *134*
Flaubert, Gustave, *French novelist*
	(1821-1880) *71*
Fleury, André Hercule de, *French cardinal*
	and politician (1653-1743) *33*
Foucault, Michel, *French philosopher*
	(1926-) *29*
FOURIER, Charles, *French writer* (1772-1837)
	67
Franco, Francisco, *Spanish dictator*
	(1892-1975) *8*
G. B. P., *see* Piranesi
G. de' D., *see* Dondi
G. E. H., *see* Haussmann
G. M., *see* Méliès
G. W. L., *see* Leibniz
Galilei, Galileo, *Italian mathematician and*
	physicist (1564-1642) *20*
Godwin, William, *English writer*
	(1756-1836) *59*
Goldoni, Carlo, *Venetian playwright*
	(1707-1793) *39*
Goncourt, Edmond and Jules Huot de,
	French writers (1822-1896 and
	1830-1870) *105*

Goya, Francisco, *Spanish painter and graphic artist* (1746-1828) *33*

GUEVARA de la Serna, Ernesto, *Argentine revolutionary* (1928-1967) *141*

Guggenheim, Daniel, *American industrialist* (1856-1930) *3*

GUILLOTIN, Joseph Ignace, *French physician* (1738-1814) *50*

GUTENBERG, Johann Gensfleisch zum, *German printer* (1395-1468) *4*

H. M. S., *see* Stanley

Haller, Albrecht von, *Swiss poet and anatomist* (1708-1777) *42*

Halley, Edmund, *English astronomer* (1656-1742) *47*

HAUSSMANN, Georges Eugène Baron, *French government official and urban planner* (1809-1891) *96*

Heine, Heinrich, *German writer* (1797-1856) *79*

Herschel, Sir William, *German astronomer* (1738-1822) *47*

Herzen, Alexander Ivanovich, *Russian writer* (1812-1870) *105*

Hobbes, Thomas, *English philosopher* (1588-1679) *90*

Hoel, Sigurd, *Norwegian writer* (1890-1960) *133*

Hoffmann, Ernst Theodor Amadeus, *German writer* (1776-1822) *85*

Huch, Ricarda, *German writer* (1864-1947) *103*

HUMBOLDT, Alexander von, *German scientist* (1769-1859) *62*

Messier, Charles, *French astronomer*
(1730-1817) *47,63*

Molotov, Vyachslav Mikhailovich, *Russian politician* (1890-   ) *131*

Mussolini, Benito, *Italian dictator*
(1883-1945) *81*

N. M., *see* Macchiavelli

Napoleon Bonaparte, *Emperor of France*
(1769-1821) *8*

Nechayev, Sergey Gennadievich, *Russian revolutionary* (1847-1882) *106*

Nettlau, Max, *Austrian social historian*
(1865-1944) *105*

Newton, Sir Isaac, *English mathematician and physicist* (1643-1727) *24,68*

Nietzsche, Friedrich, *German philosopher*
(1844-1900) *91*

Nightingale, Florence, *English nurse*
(1820-1910) *89*

Nikolai I, Pavlovich, *Russian Tsar*
(1796-1855) *100*

O. E., *see* Evans

O'Donovan, *Irish day laborer* (1829-1857) *90*

Orlov, Prince Aleksey Federovich, *Russian policeman* (1786-1861) *103*

Øverland, Arnulf, *Norwegian writer*
(1889-1968) *133*

Petrarca, Francesco, *Italian poet* (1304-1374)
1,3

Piranesi, Giovanni Battista (1720-1778) *39*

Proudhon, Pierre Joseph, *French writer*
(1809-1865) *79*

Psilanderhjelm, Petronella Sofia, née Fries
(1709-1865) *31*

R. di S., *see* Sangro

Radziwill, Prince Antoni Henryk, *landowner from Polish Lithuania* (1775-1833) *100*

Randon, Jacques César, *French military officer* (1795-1871) *83*

Ravel, Maurice, *French composer* (1875-1937) *134*

Réaumur, René Antoine de, *French naturalist* (1683-1757) *46*

REICH, Wilhelm, *psychotherapist from Austria-Hungary* (1897-1957) *133*

Reil, Johann Christian, *German physician* (1759-1813) *42,129*

ROBERT-HOUDIN, Jean Eugène, *French magician* (1805-1871) *83,123*

Rothschild, James Meyer, *banker from Germany* (1792-1868) *100*

Rudolf II, *German emperor* (1552-1612) *16*

Sahagún, *see* Bernardino

SANGRO, Raimondo di, *Prince of Sansevero, Neapolitan scholar* (1710-1771) *36*

Schmidt, Tobias, *German mechanic* (1762-1796) *51*

SEMMELWEIS, Ignaz Phillip, *Hungarian physician* (1818-1865) *108*

SPALLANZANI, Lazzaro, *Italian biologist* (1729-1799) *44*

Spinoza, Baruch de, *philosopher from Holland* (1632-1677) *24*

Stalin, Yosif Visarionovich, *dictator from Georgia* (1879-1953) *8*

STANLEY, Sir Henry Morgan, *English explorer* (1841-1904) *116*

OTHER BOOKS OF INTEREST PUBLISHED BY URIZEN

LITERATURE

Ehrenburg, Ilya
The Life of the Automobile, novel,
   192 pages
Cloth $8.95 / paper $4.95

Enzensberger, Hans Magnus
Mausoleum, poetry, 132 pages
Cloth $10.00 / paper $4.95

Hamburger, Michael
German Poetry 1910-1975, 576 pages
Cloth $17.50 / paper $6.95

Handke, Peter
Nonsense & Happiness, poetry,
   80 pages
Cloth $7.95 / paper $3.95

Hansen, Olaf (Ed.)
*The Radical Will, Randolph Bourne
(Selected Writings) 1911-1918*
   500 pages
Cloth $17.50 / paper $7.95

Innerhofer, Franz
Beautiful Days, novel, 228 pages
Cloth $8.95 / paper $4.95

Kroetz, Franz Xaver
Farmyard & Other Plays, 192 pages
Cloth $12.95 / paper $4.95

Montale, Eugenio
Poet in Our Time (essays), 96 pages
Cloth $5.95 / paper $2.95

Shepard, Sam
*Angel City, Curse of the Starving
   Class, & Other Plays,* 300 pages
Cloth $15.00 / paper $4.95

FILM

Bresson, Robert
Notes on Cinematography, 132 pages
Cloth $6.95 / paper $2.95

Bresson, Robert
The Complete Screenplays, Vol 2
   400 pages
Cloth $17.50 / paper $6.95

PSYCHOLOGY

Borneman, Ernest (Ed.)
The Psychoanalysis of Money, 420 pages
Cloth $15.00 / paper $5.95

Doerner, Klaus
Madmen and the Bourgeoisie, 384 pages
Cloth $15.00 / paper $5.95

Patrick C. Lee and Robert S. Stewart
Sex Differences, 500 pages
Cloth $17.50 / paper $5.95

Moser, Tilman
Years of Apprenticeship on the Couch,
240 pages / Cloth $10.00

ECONOMICS

De Brunhoff, Suzanne
Marx on Money, 192 pages
Cloth $10.00 / paper $4.95

Linder, Marc
Anti-Samuelson Vol. I, 400 pages
Cloth $15.00 / paper $5.95
Anti-Samuelson, Vol. II, 440 pages
Cloth $15.00 / paper $5.95

SOCIOLOGY

Andrew Arato/Eike Gebhardt (Eds.)
The Essential Frankfurt School Reader,
544 pages / Cloth $17.50 / paper $5.95

Pearce, Frank
Crimes of the Powerful, 176 pages
Paper $4.95

Van Onselen, Charles
Chibaro (African Mine Labor in Southern
Rhodesia), 368 pages / Cloth $17.50

Shaw, Martin
Marxism Versus Sociology
   (A Reading Guide), 120 pages
Cloth $6.95 / paper $2.25

Shaw, Martin
Marxism and Social Science, 125 pages
Paper $2.95

Thönnessen, Werner
The Emancipation of Women, 185 pages
Cloth $10.00 / paper $4.95

Write for a complete catalog to:
Urizen Books, Inc., 66 West Broadway, New York, N.Y. 10007